WELL, I DIDN'T KNOW THAT!

WHAT YOU CAN AND CANNOT DO
UNDER
THE RULES OF GOLF

explained in terms of:

course features
playing conditions
players' actions
players' responsibilities
and
penalties

FRANK SAWDON

MINERVA PRESS
ATLANTA LONDON SYDNEY

WELL, I DIDN'T KNOW THAT!
Copyright © Frank Sawdon 1996

ISBN 1 85863 650 7

First Published 1996 by
MINERVA PRESS
315–317 Regent Street
London W1R 7YB

2nd Impression 1997
3rd Impression 1999

Printed in Great Britain for Minerva Press

WELL, I DIDN'T KNOW THAT!

WHAT YOU CAN AND CANNOT DO
UNDER
THE RULES OF GOLF

TABLE OF CONTENTS

PLAYERS' ACTIONS

PLAYERS' RESPONSIBILITIES

INTRODUCTION

Most golfers, particularly starters, have only a minimum knowledge of the Rules of the game and this persists throughout their playing life. This situation has, moreover, been bedevilled by changes to the Rules every four years, and especially by the major revision to the Rules in 1984.

Knowledge of the Rules tends to be acquired in a haphazard fashion, usually when a Rule has been infringed. This leads, in many instances, to lengthy discussions in the clubhouse where opinions rather than facts are offered. When the Committee member responsible for the adjudication is brought into the discussion he usually has not only to read the Rule book but also a lengthy book of Decisions. Although his decision is final it is not necessarily correct.

This book looks at the Rules of the game as they apply to:

o   features of a golf course

o   playing conditions

o   players' actions

o   players' responsibilities

o   players' rights

o   penalties for infringements

It is intended to provide, in the simplest terms possible, knowledge of what a player can and cannot do:

o   in a particular situation on a golf course

o   in or on a particular feature of the course

o   in different playing conditions on the course

o   when carrying out the playing actions of the game

o   with the implements of the game

It cannot replace the Rules of Golf or the Decisions, but it is intended to enlighten players rather than for all to have to study the 43 Definitions and 34 Rules written in perfect, concise English or the 1095 Decisions which have been reached by the R&A. These cannot just be read and understood but have to be studied. In some instances the Committee Member responsible for adjudication under the Rules has used quite the wrong Rule to adjudicate on an infringement.

One of the difficulties of the study approach is that each player has to acquire a deep knowledge in order to be able to apply the correct rules to a feature.

This book is intended to reduce, if not to eliminate entirely, this barrier to the correct application of the Rules.

The majority of golfers will find something new on every page and think, "Well, I didn't know that". Hence the book's title.

Note: although some golfers consider anyone playing in a competition of any kind to be an opponent, in this book the following apply:

opponent – refers to match play

fellow competitor – refers to stroke play

partner – refers to four-ball, foursome and greensome match play
          or stroke play.

LOHIMP = loss of hole in match play
TSISP = two strokes in stroke play

1
ON THE FIRST TEE

o   General aspects of the teeing ground are given in Section 2.

o   You should be on the first tee five minutes before your tee-off time which is defined by the Committee (a starting sheet which you or the professional fill in is deemed to be blessed by the Committee).

o   You should check that you don't have more than 14 clubs. If you do, those in excess of 14 must be taken out of your bag and put in the Clubhouse or your car. Before you begin a round you cannot declare excess clubs out of play and leave them in your bag; if you do you will be disqualified.

o   You should check that your balls are uniquely identifiable and any ball which may be used as a provisional ball is marked differently to the others (see Sections 24 and 25 for the implications).

o   You should check any Local Rules that are in force. In particular, note:

       –   whether paths are obstructions or integral parts of the course
       –   whether posts (150 yard markers, in-course O.O.B. markers, hazard margin markers, direction markers, etc.) are movable or immovable obstructions. To move an immovable obstruction is penalised LOHIMP or TSISP
       –   what areas are O.O.B
       –   whether stones in bunkers have been declared to be movable obstructions.

o   If you are distracted, e.g. by other competitors approaching the tee during your backswing and you top your tee shot, you are not permitted to replay the stroke. You have to accept distractions.

LOHIMP = loss of hole in match play
TSISP = two strokes in stroke play

o   In many Clubs the first fairway and the practice range are adjacent. Before a stroke play competition, don't play a practice stroke from the first tee into the practice area. You will be disqualified unless the Committee waives the disqualification and only penalises you two strokes.

o   In match play, the side entitled to play first from the first tee is determined by lot.

o   In stroke play, the player entitled to play first from the first tee is determined by the order of the draw.

o   There is no Rule which decrees that the lowest handicap player plays first.

o   In stroke play, if, at the first tee you play out of turn there is no penalty. Don't abandon the ball and play another because you will be penalised stroke and distance. The original ball would be deemed lost.

2
ON ANY TEEING GROUND

o   The tee may be many yards in length and width but the teeing ground for a hole is a rectangular area two club lengths deep, the sides of which are defined by the outside limits of two tee markers.

o   You can use a tee peg, some sand or a surface you create to support the ball for the stroke.

o   You can take your stance outside teeing ground to take your stroke.

o   Tee markers are fixed before the first stroke on the teeing ground. Thereafter they are obstructions. If movable you can move them, but you must replace them exactly where they were.

o   Don't relocate tee markers because they are not in line, too far back or too close together – you will be disqualified.

o   If you knock the ball off the tee in addressing it, it may be re-teed without penalty since the ball is not in play.

o   If you have played a stroke at the ball and missed it and you address it again and knock it off the tee, you incur a penalty stroke and the ball must be replaced.

o   If your first stroke barely moves the ball and it is still in the teeing ground you must play it as it lies – you cannot re-tee it.

o   If visitors played the 16th rather than the 7th (adjacent holes) and teed off from the 17th before realising their error, they would be disqualified. When they played from the 17th tee they were playing from the "next teeing ground".

LOHIMP = loss of hole in match play
TSISP = two strokes in stroke play

o   If your original ball goes out of bounds from the tee and while addressing your second ball it falls off the tee there is no penalty since the ball was not in play. The ball may be re-teed.

o   In match play, if, when starting a hole, you play from outside the teeing ground, your opponent may require you to cancel the stroke so played and play a ball from within the teeing ground without penalty.

o   In stroke play, if, when starting a hole, you play from outside the teeing ground, you incur a two stroke penalty and you must play a ball from within the teeing ground.

o   In stroke play, if you play your ball from outside the teeing ground and it comes to rest out of bounds, the penalty is two strokes, not four. The ball played from outside the teeing ground was not in play. The fact that the ball came to rest out of bounds is irrelevant and the stroke did not count.

o   If you are distracted, e.g. your opponent or fellow competitor drops a ball during your backswing, and you top your tee shot, you are not permitted to replay the stroke. You have to accept distractions.

o   If you miss the ball in playing a tee shot you can still press down an irregularity in the turf behind the ball even though the ball is in play. Irregularities of surface on the teeing ground may be eliminated, whether or not the ball is in play.

o   You can break off or pull out grass growing behind a ball on the teeing ground.

o   On the teeing ground you cannot break off an overhanging tree branch which interferes with your swing. The penalty would be LOHIMP or TSISP.

LOHIMP = loss of hole in match play
TSISP = two strokes in stroke play

o   If when playing from the teeing ground you miss the ball completely, you cannot adjust the height of the tee. If you do, the penalty is one stroke and the original height of the tee must be re-set. If you played the ball from the adjusted height you would be penalised LOHIMP or a further TSISP.

o   If you make a stroke at the ball and just touch it and it falls off the tee – don't re-tee it – you would incur a penalty stroke. If you did re-tee it and play you would be penalised LOHIMP or a further TSISP.

o   If you play a provisional ball from the tee and it strikes and moves your original ball, there is no penalty and the original ball must be replaced.

o   If you miss with your first stroke and hit the ball O.O.B. with your second stroke, you can re-tee anywhere within the teeing ground for your fourth stroke.

3
IN A BUNKER

o A bunker is a hazard and therefore not part of the course which is "through the green". Grass-covered ground bordering or within a bunker is not part of the bunker. The margin of a bunker extends vertically downwards, but not upwards.

o You can use a clubhead to search for a ball which is covered by sand in a bunker.

o While searching for your ball which is covered by loose impediments or sand you can remove by probing, raking or other means as many loose impediments or as much sand as will allow you to see part of the ball.

o There is no penalty for playing a wrong ball from a bunker.

o Don't, as a gesture of sportsmanship, remove a loose impediment in a bunker which improves the lie of your opponent's ball which lies in the bunker. You would lose the hole.

o You cannot touch your ball in a bunker for identification purposes. The penalty would be one stroke for touching your ball purposely.

o In order to assist you getting into and out of a bunker, you may use a club or a cane so long as nothing is done which constitutes testing the condition of the bunker or improves the lie of the ball.

o If your ball is buried in sand in a bunker and you remove it from the buried lie during search, you must replace it and re-cover it. You may then remove as much sand as will allow you to see part of (not all) the ball.

o If your ball in a bunker is covered by leaves to the extent that it is not visible when you address it but it is visible from another angle, you cannot remove enough leaves (loose impediments) to allow you to see the ball when you address it. You can remove loose impediments covering a ball in a bunker only if the ball is not visible from any angle.

o You can ground your club on sand which has spilt over the margin of a bunker since it is not part of the bunker.

o You can ground your club on grass-covered ground within a bunker since it is not part of the bunker. Similarly with a tree in a bunker since the margin of a bunker does not extend upwards.

o If your ball lies on the edge of the bunker overhanging, but not touching, the sand, it is not in the bunker. The margin does not extend upwards.

o If your ball becomes embedded in the vertical lip of a bunker which is not grass-covered, you cannot consider the ball to be lying "through the green". Therefore you cannot declare the ball unplayable and drop the ball behind the bunker. You have to consider the ball as being in the bunker.

o If your ball is lying on a movable (rake) or immovable obstruction (rake holder) in a bunker it is considered to be in the bunker, even though the margin of a bunker does not extend vertically upwards.

o If there is a bunker between your ball and the hole, you cannot smooth footprints or other irregularities in the bunker on your line of play. Penalty is TSISP or LOHIMP.

o You can move sand in order to place your feet firmly in taking your stance but you cannot build up the sand to get a level stance.

o   A solidly embedded stone in a bunker is ground in the bunker and touching it in making your backswing is a penalty of LOHIMP or TSISP.

o   If there is a bunker between your ball and the hole and you walk through the bunker to remove a rake on your line of play, to measure the distance to the hole, etc., you cannot smooth footprints to restore the line to its original condition. You can worsen your line of play but not restore it to its original condition. Penalty TSISP or LOHIMP.

o   If there is a bunker between your ball and the hole, you may test the condition of the bunker to determine whether it is feasible to putt through it. However, such testing must not improve the line of play.

o   If there is a bunker between your ball and the hole and you decide to putt through the bunker you may remove loose impediments (twigs) in the bunker. However you cannot press down sand on your line of play if this would improve your line of play.

o   If your ball lies outside a bunker you can take your stance in the bunker and you may ground your club on the sand in the bunker or touch the sand during your backswing. However the club must be grounded only lightly.

o   When your ball is in a bunker you cannot lean on a club in the bunker while waiting for someone else to play. Penalty is TSISP or LOHIMP.

o   If you make a practice swing in a bunker, don't touch the sand. The penalty is TSISP or LOHIMP.

o   In a bunker, if a mound made by a burrowing animal interferes with your backswing, take relief. If you don't and your club touches the mound (the mound is ground in the hazard), the penalty is TSISP or LOHIMP.

LOHIMP = loss of hole in match play
TSISP = two strokes in stroke play

o   In searching for your ball in a bunker any footprints you make cannot be smoothed out until after you have played the ball. Your caddie, on his own initiative, could smooth the footprints provided the smoothing did not improve the lie of your ball.

o   If you have played your ball into a bunker and you find a ball and move a loose impediment partially covering the ball which turns out not to be your ball, you are penalised LOHIMP or TSISP.

o   If, when addressing a ball in a bunker, you accidentally touch the ball with your club but do not move it, there is no penalty.

o   If you accidentally move a loose impediment in a bunker there is no penalty provided it was not moved during your backswing or the lie of the ball or the area of the intended swing was not improved.

o   If you accidentally kick a loose impediment (pine cone, stone, etc. – see list in Section 13) into a bunker in which your ball lies, don't remove it, the penalty is TSISP or LOHIMP.

o   If you remove a loose impediment (see list in Section 13) in a bunker and your ball in the bunker moves, you are penalised three strokes. Two for moving a loose impediment and one because the ball moved. Your ball must be replaced.

o   If a divot from a partner, fellow competitor or opponent comes to rest near your ball in a bunker, you may remove it. You are entitled to the lie your stroke gave you.

o   If a pine cone falls from a tree and comes to rest near your ball in a bunker, don't remove it. This is a natural occurrence – the divot above caused the lie of the ball to be altered as a result of an act by another player.

o   If you and another player are in a bunker and you have to play second, the other player can rake out footprints or you can ask him to rake out footprints, without penalty.

o   You can place an umbrella, a rake or your clubs in the bunker without penalty.

o   Throwing a rake into a bunker in which your ball lies is permitted, unless it moves the ball, in which case you are penalised one stroke and your ball must be replaced. Placing the rake in the bunker is advised.

o   If you take a rake into a bunker in which your ball lies, don't stick the handle into the sand. You are prohibited from testing the condition of the sand.

o   You are deemed to have taken your stance in a bunker when you have shuffled your feet in the act of "digging in".

o   In a bunker you may "dig in" and take a stance without a club or you may then change the club without penalty. You are not deemed to be testing the condition of the bunker.

o   If your ball is in a bunker you cannot take a firm stance in another part of the bunker and simulate your bunker shot with or without a club. You are deemed to be testing the condition of the bunker.

o   In a bunker, if you have taken a stance with one club then decide to change clubs, you cannot smooth out the first foot marks and take a different stance.

o   In a bunker, if you accidentally touch the sand in making your backswing you are penalised TSISP or LOHIMP.

o   In a bunker, if you accidentally touch a loose impediment in making your backswing you are penalised TSISP or LOHIMP.

o   In playing from a bunker, if your club touches a bare earth wall during the backswing you are touching ground in the hazard. Penalty is TSISP or LOHIMP. You are only allowed to touch an obstruction (artificial wall). An earth wall is not an artificial wall.

o   In a bunker, if you fail to extricate the ball don't swing your club into the sand in anger. You would be penalised TSISP or LOHIMP.

o   In a bunker, if you fail to extricate the ball, you are permitted to smooth irregularities from where the ball was played if it does not improve the lie of the ball.

o   If a shot played from a bunker comes to rest out of bounds, you may smooth out the footprints at the place where the ball may be dropped. The prohibition on smoothing footprints only applies when your ball lies in or touches the bunker.

o   In a bunker, if you fail to extricate the ball, smooth your footprints and fail to extricate the ball a second time and it rolls back into the smoothed area, you incur a penalty of TSISP or LOHIMP.

o   If you take a stance to your ball in a bunker with or without a club and your ball moves, you are penalised one stroke and your ball must be replaced.

o   If, while taking your stance in a bunker the ball moves, there is no penalty, unless your approach to the ball caused it to move. In the first case the ball is played as it lies, in the second case the ball must be replaced and one penalty stroke is added.

o   In a bunker, if your ball is played by a fellow competitor or opponent, it must be replaced.

o   If, in a bunker, you are required to lift your ball because it interferes with another player's stroke, the original lie of the ball must be re-created as nearly as possible, even if it was a heel mark, and your ball placed in it.

o   If, in a bunker, the lie of your ball is altered by another player taking his stance, you can re-create your original lie as nearly as possible.

o   If, in a bunker, your ball comes to rest against a rake (movable obstruction) and it moves when the rake is moved there is no penalty. Your ball must be replaced. You cannot press the ball lightly into the sand to make it stay in position.

o   A half-eaten pear in front of your ball in a bunker cannot be removed – it is a loose impediment.

o   If your ball is in a bunker completely covered by casual water, you can play the ball as it lies or:

   (a)   drop the ball in the bunker without penalty at the nearest place not nearer the hole, where the depth of the casual water is least;

   (b)   drop the ball behind the bunker under penalty of one stroke;

   (c)   declare the ball unplayable (see options below).

o   Under the options above you cannot elect to take Option (a) and, because you don't like the result, take Option (b).

o   The maximum available relief you can take in a bunker completely covered by casual water is the spot for which either the lie or your stance is in shallower water.

o   If, when taking relief in a bunker completely covered by casual water, your ball rolls from the spot giving maximum available relief, you can re-drop it and then you can place it where it first struck the bunker when re-dropped.

LOHIMP = loss of hole in match play
TSISP = two strokes in stroke play

o   Grass banks or faces of bunkers are not "closely mown areas" unless they are cut to fairway height. If your ball is plugged in such closely mown areas you can take relief.

o   If you declare your ball unplayable in a bunker you can:

(a)   Play a ball as nearly as possible at the spot from which the original ball was last played;

(b)   Drop a ball within two club lengths of the spot where the ball lay, but not nearer the hole AND in the bunker;

(c)   Drop a ball behind the point where the ball lay, keeping that point directly between the hole and the spot on which the ball is dropped, with no limit to how far behind that point the ball can be dropped as long as it is in the bunker.

o   If you declare your ball unplayable in a bunker and you lift the ball, you cannot remove loose impediments because your ball no longer lies in the bunker. The penalty is LOHIMP or TSISP. You may elect to take relief by dropping in the bunker.

o   If, through the green, you declare your ball unplayable, in obtaining relief you can drop your ball in a bunker.

LOHIMP = loss of hole in match play
TSISP = two strokes in stroke play

4
IN A WATER HAZARD

o   Don't, as a gesture of sportsmanship, remove a loose impediment in a water hazard which improves your opponent's lie in the water hazard. You would lose the hole.

o   In a water hazard, if your ball is covered by loose impediments (leaves) so that it is not visible when you address it, but it is visible from another angle, you cannot remove sufficient loose impediments to allow you to see the ball when you address it. The ball does not have to be visible from any angle.

o   If you intend to putt through a water hazard when your ball lies outside the water hazard, you can remove a loose impediment in the water hazard if it is in your line of play.

o   Don't take practice swings in a water hazard – you might touch the ground and be penalised LOHIMP or TSISP.

o   In order to assist you getting into and out of a water hazard, you can use a club or a cane so long as nothing is done which constitutes testing the condition of the water hazard or improves the lie of the ball.

o   You can take a practice swing and touch grass in a water hazard and there would be no penalty provided that you did not improve your lie or test the condition of the hazard.

o   A solidly embedded stone in a water hazard is ground in the hazard and touching it in making your backswing is a penalty of LOHIMP or TSISP.

o   If your ball is lost in either a water hazard or the casual water overflowing the water hazard, you must assume it is lost in the water hazard.

LOHIMP = loss of hole in match play
TSISP = two strokes in stroke play

o   If your ball lies in a water hazard, don't rotate it to identify it. You would incur a penalty stroke.

o   If your ball is lying in a water hazard and you accidentally touch it when addressing it but without moving it, there is no penalty.

o   If your ball is lying in a water hazard and a ball is partially covered by a loose impediment, don't remove the loose impediment for the purpose of identification. Even if the ball is not yours you are penalised LOHIMP or TSISP.

o   As above, if you decide to lift and drop your ball outside the hazard, you are still penalised if you remove a loose impediment.

o   If you accidentally move a loose impediment in a water hazard there is no penalty, provided the loose impediment was not moved in making the backswing and the lie of the ball or area of intended swing was not improved.

o   If you move a loose impediment in a water hazard and your ball moves, you are penalised three strokes in stroke play; two for moving a loose impediment and one because the ball moved. The ball must be replaced.

o   If your ball is in a water hazard and the divot of your partner, fellow competitor or opponent comes to rest near your ball you can remove the divot. You are entitled to the lie which your stroke gave you.

o   You may place your umbrella or your bag of clubs in a water hazard, provided nothing is done which may constitute testing the soil or improving the lie of the ball.

o   When your ball lies in a water hazard, don't take practice swings. If you touch the ground or bend a shrub which improves the area of your intended swing the penalty is LOHIMP or TSISP.

o   If your ball lies in a water hazard, but close to the line defining the margin of the hazard, you may ground your club outside the hazard.

o   You may ground your club on a bridge over a water hazard. The bridge is an obstruction and not "ground in the water hazard".

o   If your ball lies in running water in a water hazard and the ball moves after you have addressed it and you play it while it is moving, there is no penalty.

o   If two balls are in a water hazard and they are exchanged after recovery, there is no penalty. You have to drop "a ball", thus allowing a substitution.

o   You cannot declare your ball unplayable in a water hazard.

o   If your ball is lost in an underground drainpipe or culvert (an immovable obstruction) in a water hazard, a ball may be dropped in the water hazard without penalty.

o   If a pond has overflowed, the overflow is casual water if it is outside the margin of the hazard.

o   If a stake defining the margin of a water hazard has been removed, the hole in which the stake was previously located is a hole made by a greenkeeper, but such a hole is in the hazard.

o   A ball is in a water hazard when some part of the ball breaks the plane of the margin extended vertically upwards, even though the ball does not touch the ground or grass inside the hazard.

o   If the stakes in a water hazard have been improperly installed and your ball is outside the line of stakes but obviously in the water hazard you cannot claim it to be in casual water. The natural boundary of the water hazard should be recognised.

o   A reservoir is a water hazard.

o   If you cannot identify your ball in a water hazard and you play it and lose it – you must assume it was your ball.

o   If you assume your ball is in a water hazard and play from where the original ball was played, the ball you play is in play under stroke and distance penalty and the original ball is lost – even if it is subsequently found outside the water hazard.

o   If your ball appears to have come to rest in a water hazard and you play another ball under stroke and distance penalty but your original ball is found outside the water hazard, it is lost and the second ball is in play.

o   "Reasonable evidence" means that the evidence must be preponderantly in favour of the ball being in the water hazard, otherwise the ball must be considered lost outside the water hazard. Splashing does not necessarily mean the ball stayed in the hazard.

o   If there is "reasonable evidence" that your ball was in a water hazard and was lost and you proceed to drop a ball outside the water hazard, that ball becomes the ball in play. If your original ball is subsequently found outside the water hazard it has to be abandoned.

     If there is not "reasonable evidence" that your ball was in a water hazard, you cannot drop a ball outside the water hazard since it would be in the wrong place, the penalty for which is LOHIMP. In stroke play the penalty is stroke and distance plus two strokes for playing from the wrong place. If the breach was a serious one you would be subject to disqualification unless you corrected the error.

o   If you play out of a bunker into a water hazard and the ball is not playable you may, under penalty of one stroke:

LOHIMP = loss of hole in match play
TSISP = two strokes in stroke play

    (a)   drop a ball behind the water hazard

    (b)   drop a ball in the bunker at the spot you originally played from.

o   If your ball is lying in a water hazard and your caddie lifts it without your authority you are penalised one stroke. You may either replace the ball or drop a ball outside the water hazard and incur an additional penalty stroke.

o   If you play out of a water hazard into an out of bounds area, you may drop in a ball in the water hazard or, under further penalty of one stroke, drop a ball outside the water hazard.

o   Don't treat a water hazard as a lateral water hazard if your ball has spun back into the water hazard – if you do, you are penalised LOHIMP. In stroke play you are penalised one stroke for taking relief plus a further two strokes for playing from a wrong place and you must rectify the error or you would be disqualified.

o   If your tee shot might be lost in a water hazard you cannot play a provisional ball. If you play another ball it is in play.

o   If your ball might be lost outside a water hazard or out of bounds yet it is in the water hazard you may play a provisional ball. If the original ball is found in the hazard the provisional ball must be abandoned.

o   If, through the green, you declare your ball unplayable, in taking relief you can drop the ball in a water hazard.

5
IN A LATERAL WATER HAZARD

o   A ditch with O.O.B. on one side is automatically a lateral water hazard.

o   If your ball pitches on the far side of a ditch and spins back into the ditch, don't treat it as a lateral water hazard and drop on the far side of the ditch; the penalty would be LOHIMP. In stroke play you are penalised one stroke for taking relief plus a further two strokes for playing from a wrong place and the error must be rectified or you would be disqualified.

o   If it is not possible to drop your ball further from the hole than the position it last crossed a lateral water hazard, the only options for relief are to take the stroke and distance penalty or to drop a ball across the lateral water hazard.

o   If your ball crosses water where it is marked as a water hazard but comes to rest in water marked as a lateral water hazard, you can only proceed as if the water is a water hazard.

o   In stroke play, if you and one of your fellow competitors think your ball crossed the margin of a lateral water hazard in a certain position and you drop a ball at that point, that ball is in play. If another fellow competitor disagrees with your assessment and finds your ball some yards behind in the lateral water hazard, you can lift your ball in play, in the wrong place, and re-drop it. You cannot play the ball in the lateral water hazard.

If you had played the ball from the wrong place there would be no penalty since it was done as a result of your assessment.

o   If two balls are hit into a lateral water hazard the ball furthest from the hole in the hazard plays first. The fact that the other ball has crossed the margin farther from the hole does not count.

LOHIMP = loss of hole in match play
TSISP = two strokes in stroke play

If both balls above are lost – the order of play should be decided by lot, as if the balls were equidistant from the hole.

6
ON THE GREEN

o   You can repair damage to the putting green made by golf shoe spikes only on completion of the hole.

o   If your ball is on the lip of the hole, don't putt it one handed and catch the ball with your other hand. The penalty would be LOHIMP or TSISP. In order for the ball to be holed it must be at rest within the circumference of the hole.

o   When replacing your ball on the putting green you are advised to place the ball on the spot from which it was lifted. Placing the ball in front of the ball marker and rolling or sliding it into the place from which it was lifted is allowed but not recommended, since it could be construed as doing something which might influence the movement of the ball when played, e.g. pressing down a raised tuft of grass.

o   On the green you cannot lay your bag parallel to the line of putt to shield the line from the wind. Penalty is LOHIMP or TSISP.

o   On the green, if you believe another player's ball will strike the flagstick lying on the green, don't move it. If you do you are penalised LOHIMP or TSISP.

o   If your ball overhangs the lip of the hole, don't jump close to the hole in the hope of jarring the earth and causing the ball to fall into the hole. You would be penalised LOHIMP or TSISP if the ball was still moving. If the ball was at rest you would incur a penalty of one stroke and the ball would have to be replaced.

If there was doubt as to whether the ball was moving or not it would be presumed to be moving.

LOHIMP = loss of hole in match play
TSISP = two strokes in stroke play

o   In match play, don't agree in advance to concede short putts, you and your opponent would be disqualified. You can only concede the "next stroke" and it cannot be conceded in advance.

o   On the green don't agree with an opponent or fellow competitor to repair spike marks on one another's line of putt. You would both be disqualified for agreeing to touch the line of putt.

o   If your ball lies near the hole and in a position to assist a fellow competitor whose ball lies off the green and you intend to mark and lift it and state your intention to do so, but your fellow competitor plays before you have the opportunity to lift it and his ball strikes your ball he is disqualified.

o   When you have marked and lifted your ball on the green don't take practice putts with it on or off the green. Penalty is LOHIMP or TSISP.

o   When you have marked and lifted your ball on the green check when replacing it that it is the same ball. If by mistake you substitute and play another ball the ball is not a wrong ball but the ball in play, and you are penalised LOHIMP or TSISP.

o   Your ball is on the putting green when any part of it touches the putting green.

o   If your ball lies off the green, overhanging but not touching the green, but a clump of mud adhering to the ball touches the green, your ball is not on the green.

o   If your ball lies on the green you cannot brush aside casual water on your line of putt or mop it up with a towel. Penalty would be LOHIMP or TSISP.

o   If your ball lies on the green you cannot brush dew or frost from your line of putt. Dew or frost are not loose impediments. Penalty is LOHIMP or TSISP.

30

LOHIMP = loss of hole in match play
TSISP = two strokes in stroke play

o   If you remove an embedded acorn from your line of putt you cannot repair the indentation it has left. The penalty for so doing would be LOHIMP or TSISP.

o   If your ball lies on the green you are entitled to brush aside loose impediments from your line of putt with your hand or a club. If you use your cap or a towel the penalty is LOHIMP or TSISP.

o   Excessive use of your hand to brush away leaves on your line of putt is penalised LOHIMP or TSISP. "Excessive" would be a dozen strokes with the whole palm of your hand.

o   When removing loose impediments from your line of putt with a putter try to brush across the line. A minor movement of the putter down the line is not a penalty but it might be construed as influencing your ball when played.

o   If there is a tuft of grass on your line of putt and you wish to determine if it is loose or attached, you can brush the tuft lightly. If the tuft is attached and you alter its position slightly, you must restore the tuft to its original position before playing your next stroke.

o   If you intentionally walk on your line of putt the penalty is LOHIMP or TSISP. If you accidentally walk on your line of putt and the act does not improve the line, there is no penalty.

o   If an opponent or fellow competitor accidentally treads on your line of putt there is no penalty.

o   If you step on a ball mark in the act of repairing it and incidentally press down a spike mark on your line of putt the penalty is LOHIMP or TSISP.

o   If you step on an old hole plug, which is raised on your line of putt, in order to make it level with the surface of the putting green and in so doing press down a spike mark within the hole plug, there is no penalty. You can step on the line of putt in repairing old hole plugs. If the spike mark had been near but not on the hole plug you would have been penalised LOHIMP or TSISP.

o   If you have lifted, cleaned and replaced your ball on the putting green and before playing your next stroke you fear the ball might move, you can mark and lift the ball again. The ball on the green can be lifted for any reason.

o   You can re-repair a repaired ball mark on your line of putt if it is clearly identifiable as a ball mark.

o   If your ball is off the putting green but there is a ball mark on your line of play, if it is on the green you can repair it; if it is off the green you cannot; and if it is half on and half off you can repair it since it would be impractical to repair only that part which was on the green.

o   In match play, if your opponent, whose turn it is to play, requests you not to repair your pitch mark until after he has played, you cannot repair it. Penalty would be LOH.

o   You may attempt to raise or lower an old hole plug on the green to make it level with the surface.

o   If your ball lies on or near the putting green you cannot tap down spike marks on the green since this might assist you in the subsequent play of the hole.

o   In match play, if, after conceding a putt you casually pick up and roll your opponent's ball or knock it back with your putter, you are not considered to be testing the surface of the green.

o   If you have marked your ball on the green and set it aside, it is legal, but not recommended, to use your putter to roll the ball to replace it. It might be construed that you were testing the surface.

o   You can place the palm of your hand on the putting green behind your ball to determine if the green is wet. If you touched the line of putt you would be penalised LOHIMP or TSISP.

o   You may clean your ball by rubbing it on the putting green, provided the act is not for the purpose of testing the surface. Of course, it is not a recommended act.

o   The line of putt is not necessarily a straight line, but the line the ball, if properly struck, would take to go in the hole.

o   In match play, if your opponent's putt comes to rest overhanging the hole, don't be too hasty in conceding the next stroke and knocking the ball away. Your opponent is allowed ten seconds after reaching the hole to determine if the ball is at rest. Your action would cost you the hole.

o   If your stroke to the green strikes the flagstick, which has been blown down by the wind, there is no penalty since it had not been removed with your authority.

o   If your ball is lying on the putting green and it is oscillating due to wind, you cannot press it into the green to stop it oscillating. You would be deemed to have moved the ball and also have altered the original lie. If you played the ball having so moved it you would be penalised LOHIMP or TSISP.

o   If you rotate the ball to align the trademark with the hole, make sure you mark the ball first. If you don't you will be penalised one stroke.

o   If you have addressed the ball, moved away, marked and lifted your ball and it moves after you have replaced it, but not addressed it, there is no penalty. The ball must be played as it lies.

o   If your ball is on the lip of the hole and the time limit (time to walk to the hole plus ten seconds) has expired, and after addressing it, it falls into the hole, you are penalised one stroke and the ball is deemed to have been holed with your last stroke.

   If the time limit had not expired you incur a penalty of one stroke and the ball must be replaced.

o   If you accidentally move your ball on the putting green with your foot in the process of removing a loose impediment, you are penalised one stroke and the ball must be replaced. (The act of moving the ball was not directly due to the removal of the loose impediment).

o   If an insect alights onto your ball, on the putting green, after you have addressed it and the ball moves when you attempt to remove the insect, there is no penalty and the ball must be replaced.

o   Your ball is played from off the green and is in motion about a foot from the hole when it is moved by a dog to a spot ten feet from the hole. If the ball was deflected it is played as it lies, without penalty. If the ball was picked up and carried you should place the ball, without penalty, as near as possible to the spot where the original ball was when the dog picked it up.

o   Your ball is putted on the green and while it is in motion, if it is picked up or deflected by a dog the stroke is cancelled and the ball replaced.

o   If your ball is putted on the green and while it is in motion a ball played at another hole strikes it and knocks it into a bunker, you cancel the stroke and replace the ball. The other ball is a moving outside agency.

o   If your ball is putted on the green and it strikes a ball which has been lifted and set aside, there is no penalty in stroke play and the ball is played as it lies. There is no penalty in match play and the

34

ball is either played as it lies or you can cancel and replay the stroke.

o   If your ball is putted on the green and a ball which has accidentally been dropped after you have played your stroke strikes it - in match play you either play the ball as it lies or you cancel and replay the stroke without penalty - in stroke play you must cancel and replay your stroke without penalty.

The ball accidentally dropped was a moving outside agency.

o   If you have been called through and a ball from the match in front lies on the green and, while putting your ball strikes it, you are penalised TSISP. There is no penalty in match play.

o   If you putt on the green and your ball comes to rest touching another ball, but does not move it, there is no penalty. Your ball was not deflected or stopped by the other ball on the green.

o   In match play, don't mark and lift your opponent's ball without his authority. The penalty is one stroke.

If, in a similar situation, it is your ball that has been marked and lifted, remember it is only a one stroke penalty and not loss of hole. If you pick up the marker and claim the hole you will be penalised one stroke and you must replace your ball and hole out.

o   In stroke play if a fellow competitor lifts your ball without authority, there is no penalty but you must replace the ball.

o   When you have marked your ball on the green make sure you don't tread on the marker and move it – you would incur a penalty stroke.

If the marker is moved when you tap it down with your putter, there is no penalty. In this case the marker was moved accidentally in the process of lifting the ball or marking its position.

o   Make sure you have won the hole in match play. If you lift the marker and you haven't won the hole, you would be penalised one stroke.

o   If you have marked and lifted your ball on the green to let a following match through and the marker is moved by that match, you place your ball as near as possible to where it lay on the green – without penalty.

o   If your ball marker on the green may assist another player you can move it despite their request that you leave it.

o   Although not recommended, you can mark the position of your ball with the toe of a club prior to lifting it.

o   If you drop your putter on the ball and move it as you approach it to mark and lift it, you incur a penalty of one stroke. The movement of the ball was not caused by the act of marking or lifting the ball.

o   If you accidentally drop a ball marker and it strikes and moves your ball you are penalised one stroke and your ball must be replaced.

o   It is permissible, but not recommended, to mark the position of your ball on the green by scratching a line with a tee peg. Marking the green in this way causes damage.

o   If a player uses a tee peg to mark the position of his ball on the green and your ball is deflected by it when you putt, you must play the ball as it lies without penalty.

o   The position of your ball can be marked with a flower although this is inadvisable since the flower may be blown away.

LOHIMP = loss of hole in match play
TSISP = two strokes in stroke play

o   When marking the position of the ball on the green, there is no restriction on where the marker is placed. It could be placed in front of the ball, but if you do something which might influence the movement of the ball when played there is a penalty of LOHIMP or TSISP.

o   Don't mark the position of the ball by placing the ball marker two or more inches behind the ball. You cannot be considered to have marked the position of your ball with sufficient accuracy. The penalty is one stroke and the ball must be placed as near as possible to the spot from which it was lifted. If the marking was done to ensure the ball was not moved, this is unnecessary since no penalty is incurred if the ball is moved accidentally in the process of marking or lifting it.

o   Don't use a blemish on the green as a ball marker. This does not constitute marking the ball before lifting it, thus incurring a one stroke penalty.

o   After marking your ball on the green, you can knock it away rather than lift it. There is no penalty unless it is deemed to be testing the surface or playing a practice stroke.

o   There is no penalty if the ball is accidentally moved while removing the ball marker. The ball must be replaced.

o   You may align the trademark of the ball along the line of putt when you replace it.

o   A ball is in play when it is replaced, whether or not the marker has been removed. If wind moves a ball in such a situation, the ball must be played from its new position.

o   If you putt from the wrong place on the green you incur a penalty of two strokes. The score with the ball played from the wrong place counts. You are not required to correct the error by playing from the right place.

LOHIMP = loss of hole in match play
TSISP = two strokes in stroke play

o   On the line of putt, loose impediments may only be picked up or brushed aside with the hand or a club without pressing down.

o   On the green, casual water may be visible when you walk beside the line of putt but if it is not visible when you take your stance then there is no relief.

o   An aeration hole on the green is not G.U.R.

o   A sunken hole plug on the green is not G.U.R. – it can be raised to the level of the green.

o   If your ball lies off the green and casual water intervenes between your ball and the hole, there is no relief.

o   If your ball is on the green and you therefore are entitled to relief from casual water, if the nearest position affording relief which is not nearer the hole or in a hazard is off the green in the rough you must place the ball in the rough.

7
THE HOLE

o   Your ball is "holed" when it is at rest within the circumference of the hole and all of it is below the level of the lip of the hole.

o   After holing out you cannot repair any damage to the hole until your opponent, fellow competitor or partner has holed out or picked up. If you do, you incur a penalty of LOHIMP for influencing the movement of the opponent's ball or TSISP for influencing the movement of your fellow competitor's or partner's ball.

In a four ball competition your partner would be penalised.

o   In match play, if your opponent concedes your next stroke for a four and, in the process of knocking your ball back to you, inadvertently knocks it into the hole you have not then holed the ball in three. When your opponent conceded your four you had completed the hole.

o   In match play, if your opponent concedes your next stroke for a four, after the elapse of time allowed for your ball overhanging the hole you have scored a four, even if your ball falls into the hole after the concession.

o   In match play, make sure your opponent has conceded your next stroke. If you lift your ball and your opponent says it was not conceded you incur a penalty of one stroke and you must replace the ball as near as possible to where it lay.

o   In match play make sure you have won the hole after putting out before you lift your opponent's ball. If not you will be penalised one stroke for moving your opponent's ball and your opponent must replace his ball. He then has an additional stroke for the hole.

LOHIMP = loss of hole in match play
TSISP = two strokes in stroke play

o   If you lift your opponent's ball marker when you haven't won the hole you are penalised one stroke. If your opponent had a putt for a half, the hole is halved.

o   If your next stroke is conceded there is no penalty for trying to hole out unless the act would be of assistance to a partner in a four-ball or best-ball match. Your partner would then be disqualified for the hole.

o   If your next stroke is conceded and you attempt to hole out and fail, your score is that which the concession gave you and you had completed the hole.

o   A hole is completed, therefore allowing practice:

    (i)   singles match play – when you have holed out, your next stroke has been conceded or you have conceded the hole

    (ii)   individual stroke play – when you have holed out

    (iii) 4-ball match play – when both you and your partner have holed out, your next strokes have been conceded or your side has conceded the hole

    (iv) 4-ball stroke play – when both you and your partner have holed out or picked up.

    (v)   Bogey, Par and Stableford - when you have holed out or picked up.

o   In match play if your opponent holes out and has won the hole and your ball is in a bunker, you may play out of the bunker without incurring a penalty. The stroke is deemed not to be a practice stroke.

o   In match play if you give wrong information and your opponent lifts his ball marker before you correct your error, you have lost the hole. The act of lifting his marker is the equivalent of your opponent playing his next stroke.

o   In match play, if your opponent requests you to mark your ball, do so. Don't putt out. Your opponent could request you to replace your ball, without penalty, and play in correct order.

o   If your ball embeds in the side of the hole and all of it is below the level of the lip of the hole, it is considered holed though all of it is not within the circumference of the hole as required by the definition of "holed".

o   If your ball embeds in the side of the hole and part of it is above the level of the lip it is not holed. You may play the ball as it lies or lift the ball, repair the damage, and place the ball on the lip of the hole.

o   If your ball strikes the rim of a hole liner which had not been sunk deep enough and bounces out of the hole, your ball is not considered holed.

o   Your ball is holed even if it is not absolutely at rest within the hole when you pick it up. The words "at rest" in the definition of "holed" are to make it clear that if a ball falls below the lip and thereafter bounces out, it is not holed.

o   You may repair material damage to the hole before you putt if the damage is caused by a ball mark.

o   If the proper dimensions of the hole have been changed materially by other than a ball mark the Committee should be called to have the hole repaired. If the proper dimensions haven't been changed materially you should continue play without repairing the hole. If you touch the hole the penalty is LOHIMP or TSISP.

LOHIMP = loss of hole in match play
TSISP = two strokes in stroke play

o   If your ball overhangs the edge of the hole and you wait longer than the time allowance and it then falls into the hole you are subject to a one stroke penalty.

o   If your ball is overhanging the hole, you may cast a shadow on it in the hope that this will cause your ball to fall into the hole, but it must do so within the time allowance.

o   You are deemed to be standing near the hole if you are close enough to touch the flagstick, therefore you are deemed to be attending the flagstick.

o   If you play a stroke on the putting green with the flagstick in the hole, it is impossible for the ball not to touch the flagstick if it goes into the hole.

o   You can use a club to mark the position of the hole, but it then is treated as the flagstick.

o   If you hole your tee shot with a provisional ball, after your first ball may be O.O.B. or lost, that ball becomes the ball in play when you lift it out of the hole, provided that your original ball has not been found in bounds within five minutes of a search having started.

8
THE FLAGSTICK

o   When attending the flagstick, test to make sure that it can be removed from the hole easily.

o   When attending the flagstick, hold the flag still if it is fluttering in the wind.

o   When you remove the flagstick from the hole, place it on the green, don't throw it or drop it.

o   The flagstick is a movable obstruction, with or without bunting or other material attached, centred in the hole to show its position.

o   You can have the flagstick held aloft to indicate the position of a blind hole.

o   You can leave the flagstick as it is or centred in the hole. You cannot adjust it to a more favourable position than centred.

o   If your ball lodges in the flag attached to the flagstick, the ball can be placed on the lip of the hole. The flagstick is a movable obstruction.

o   If the hole liner is removed when the flagstick is removed and your ball goes into the hole there is no penalty. A hole need not contain a lining.

o   If your ball strikes the hole liner which has come out of the hole attached to the flagstick and the hole liner was moving at the time, the stroke is cancelled and the ball must be replaced. If the liner was stationary the ball must be played as it lies. The hole liner is an outside agency.

o   If, after you have putted, the flagstick attendant removes the flagstick and a knob attached to the top of the flagstick falls off and strikes your moving ball, your stroke is cancelled and the ball must be replaced. The knob is an outside agency.

o   If an opponent or fellow competitor declines to hold the flagstick upon your request you have no redress.

o   A referee or observer should not attend the flagstick. You incur no penalty, however, if you request a referee to attend it. A marker may attend the flagstick even though he is not a fellow competitor.

o   A person attending the flagstick can stand immediately behind the hole to avoid standing on another player's line.

o   You can remove the flagstick from the hole and hold it behind the hole resting on the green but this is not advised due to the possibility of damage to the green.

o   You can hold the flagstick out of the hole with one hand and putt one-handed with the other.

o   If you play a stroke from on the green with the flagstick in the hole, the ball cannot come to rest in the hole without touching the flagstick. Penalty is LOHIMP or TSISP.

o   If your ball played on the green strikes the flagstick lying on the green you incur a penalty of LOHIMP or TSISP.

o   If your ball played from off the green strikes the flagstick lying on the green there is no penalty.

o   If your ball played from off the green strikes the flagstick attendant or the flagstick when the attendant is your caddie, your partner's caddie or your partner, you incur a penalty of LOHIMP

LOHIMP = loss of hole in match play
TSISP = two strokes in stroke play

or TSISP. This is true even if you did not expressly request the flagstick to be attended.

o   If your ball strikes the flag when the flagstick is being attended there is a penalty of LOHIMP or TSISP.

o   If your ball is resting against the flagstick but is not holed and you lift it you incur a one stroke penalty and the ball must be replaced. You can then remove the flagstick.

o   In a match if you play from off the green and your ball comes to rest against the flagstick and your opponent concedes your next stroke, he is penalised one stroke for "touching" your ball. The ball must be replaced and then you can remove the flagstick.

o   If your ball comes to rest against the flagstick and, without your authority, your opponent or fellow competitor removes the flagstick and the ball moves away, your opponent is penalised one stroke, your fellow competitor is not penalised and you must replace the ball against the flagstick. You can then move or remove the flagstick.

o   If you accidentally drop the flagstick and it moves your ball you incur a penalty of one stroke and the ball must be replaced, unless you were using the flagstick for measuring.

LOHIMP = loss of hole in match play
TSISP = two strokes in stroke play

9
THE COURSE

o   The course is the whole area within which play is permitted and consists of:

  – teeing grounds
  – putting greens
  – bunkers
  – water hazards and lateral water hazards
  – areas defined as through the green
  – G.U.R.
  – paths and roads – which may be obstructions or integral parts of the course

o   Take care of the course by carefully replacing divots and by ensuring that divots are not taken when you make a practice swing.

o   Information as to the length of a hole is not advice, it is factual information available to all players through score cards, tee signs, etc.

o   You can ask anyone the distance from a permanent object, e.g. tree, bunker etc. to the centre of the green. You can only ask your partner or caddie to inform you of the distance from a non permanent object, e.g. your ball, to the putting green.

o   You can enquire as to the accuracy of the placing of a 150 yard marker and whether the distance is to the centre of the green or the front.

o   If your ball is half buried in the rough, inform your opponent or fellow competitor that you need to rotate it for identification purposes, then mark its position before so doing. If you rotate it before marking you incur a penalty of one stroke.

LOHIMP = loss of hole in match play
TSISP = two strokes in stroke play

o   If, through the green, your line of play is affected by a pitch mark made after your ball came to rest, you may repair it. If the pitch mark was there before your ball came to rest, you are not entitled to relief without penalty.

o   If, through the green, another player deposits sand on or around your ball due to a bunker shot, you are entitled to remove the sand deposited by the stroke, lift your ball and clean it without penalty.

10
OUT OF BOUNDS

o   When Out Of Bounds (O.O.B.) is defined by reference to stakes or a fence or as being beyond stakes or a fence, the O.O.B. line is determined by the nearest inside points of the stakes or fence posts at ground level excluding angled supports.

When O.O.B. is defined by a line on the ground, the line itself is O.O.B.

The O.O.B. line extends vertically upwards and downwards.

Your ball is O.O.B. when all of it is O.O.B.

You may stand O.O.B. to play a ball lying within bounds.

o   Objects such as stakes or lines defining O.O.B. are fixed. If you remove a stake, so improving the position of your ball by moving something fixed, the penalty is LOHIMP or TSISP.

o   If you play a stroke at your ball which is lying O.O.B. you are playing a ball which is not in play and therefore a wrong ball. The penalty is LOHIMP or TSISP and you must proceed under the additional stroke and distance penalty.

o   If you hit a wrong ball O.O.B. and drop another ball, then find your ball in bounds you are penalised LOHIMP or TSISP and you are obliged to hole out with your original ball. Dropping and playing another ball after hitting the wrong ball O.O.B. is a continuation of the play with that wrong ball.

o   If your swing is interfered with by an O.O.B. stake you cannot treat the stake as an obstruction and lift and drop your ball. The penalty is one stroke and the ball must be replaced otherwise the penalty is LOHIMP or TSISP.

LOHIMP = loss of hole in match play
TSISP = two strokes in stroke play

o   In stroke play, if you hit your tee shot into a practice area and, thinking it is O.O.B., lift the ball and play another stroke from the tee then discover the practice area is in play, you are penalised two strokes for lifting your ball in play and failing to replace it.

o   If your ball is lying on a slope and after you have addressed it, it moves and comes to rest O.O.B., you incur a one stroke penalty and the ball must be replaced.

o   If your ball accidentally strikes your caddie, who is standing in-bounds and the ball comes to rest O.O.B. the penalty is LOHIMP or TSISP and since the ball lies O.O.B. you incur another penalty stroke and the distance penalty.

o   If your ball accidentally strikes your caddie who is standing O.O.B. and comes to rest in bounds the penalty is LOHIMP or TSISP and since the ball is in bounds it is in play.

o   If your ball accidentally strikes your caddie who is standing O.O.B. and comes to rest O.O.B., the penalty is LOHIMP or TSISP and since the ball lies O.O.B. you incur another penalty stroke and the distance penalty.

o   If your ball accidentally strikes your opponent who is standing O.O.B. and it comes to rest O.O.B., there is no penalty and you can replay the stroke.

o   You may remove a loose impediment which is lying O.O.B. if it interferes with your stance.

o   Concrete bases of a boundary fence are not obstructions since such a base is part of the fence.

o   If a part of a boundary fence is bowed towards the course so that it is inside the boundary line formed by the fence posts, it cannot be treated as an obstruction.

LOHIMP = loss of hole in match play
TSISP = two strokes in stroke play

o   If your ball goes O.O.B. but enters an animal burrow and comes to rest in bounds, you may drop a ball, without penalty, within one club length of the point on the ground directly above its position in the burrow.

o   If your ball in bounds enters an animal burrow and comes to rest O.O.B. it is O.O.B.

o   If the flow of water in a water hazard carries your ball O.O.B. you incur the stroke and distance penalty. Water is not an outside agency.

o   If your ball may be in a water hazard you can still play a provisional ball if the ball might also be lost outside the water hazard or O.O.B. If the ball is found in the water hazard the provisional ball must be abandoned.

o   If you play a provisional ball because your original ball may be O.O.B. you must check the status of the original ball before playing the provisional ball from a position closer to the hole than the original ball. If the original ball is in bounds, your play of the provisional ball is then play with a wrong ball, the penalty for which is LOHIMP or TSISP and you would be required to hole out with the original ball.

o   If your original ball from the tee and a provisional ball are found O.O.B., your next stroke from the tee is your fifth.

11
GROUND UNDER REPAIR

o Ground Under Repair (G.U.R.) is any portion of the course so marked by order of the Committee. Stakes and lines defining G.U.R. are in such ground. The margin of G.U.R. extends vertically downwards, but not upwards.

o Relief from G.U.R. through the green is one club length from the point nearest to where the ball lies which is not nearer the hole, avoids interference by the condition and is not in a bunker, water hazard or on a putting green.

o Relief from G.U.R. in a bunker or water hazard can be taken (a) without penalty in the bunker or water hazard as near as possible to the spot where the ball lies, but not nearer the hole; (b) under penalty of one stroke outside the bunker or water hazard by dropping a ball on the line of the hole and the spot where the ball lay, with no limit to how far behind the bunker or water hazard the ball may be dropped.

o If your ball is in G.U.R. together with another ball, the ball furthest from the hole before relief is taken plays first.

o If you play your ball from G.U.R. without knowing it is G.U.R., don't pick it up and proceed under the G.U.R. Rule if you are then informed it is G.U.R. When you played out of the G.U.R., which is permissible, your ball was in play.

o If you take relief from G.U.R. and, when dropped, the ball remains outside the G.U.R. but it rolls to a position where you would have to stand in the G.U.R. to play it, you must re-drop.

o A tree which has fallen down and is being sawn for removal is G.U.R.

o   A ball lost in a tree in G.U.R. is not in the G.U.R. The margin of G.U.R. does not extend vertically upwards.

o   Grass cuttings are only G.U.R. if they are piled for removal.

o   Cracks in the earth which occur in summer are not automatically G.U.R., they have to be declared such by the Committee.

o   A hole made by a greenkeeper consisting of ground temporarily dug up in connection with course maintenance is G.U.R.

o   Aeration holes are not G.U.R.

o   A rut made by a tractor is not automatically G.U.R. It must be declared as such by the Committee.

o   An old hole plug is not G.U.R. If your ball is in one the plug can be repaired.

o   If the stake defining a margin of a water hazard has been removed, the hole is G.U.R., but it is in the water hazard.

o   In obtaining relief from G.U.R., the term "point on the course nearest to where the ball lies" means the specific point on the course (not nearer the hole, nor on a putting green nor in a hazard) nearest to which the ball originally lay at which, if the ball were so positioned, interference would cease to exist.

o   In obtaining relief from G.U.R. it is possible to improve your line of play, e.g. by avoiding playing over a bunker. This is considered your good fortune.

o   If your ball lies in casual water in an area of G.U.R. you can take relief (a) from the casual water first, drop the ball in the G.U.R. and then either play the ball as it lies or take relief from the G.U.R.; (b) from the G.U.R. first and then the casual water.

o   If, in taking relief from an unplayable lie, you drop your ball in G.U.R. from which play was prohibited, you must then take the mandatory relief from the G.U.R.

o   If there is no single point of relief nearest to where the ball lies you can choose either point from which to measure the place to drop within one club length.

o   If your ball comes to rest in pine needles piled for removal you can remove the pine needles (loose impediments) or treat them as G.U.R. If the position of your ball after dropping from the G.U.R. is such that the pine needles intervene with your line of play, they must then be treated as loose impediments.

o   Make sure your ball is lost in G.U.R. before claiming it is. If you proceed as if it is, then find your ball outside the G.U.R., you would be penalised LOHIMP. In stroke play you would be penalised stroke and distance plus two strokes for playing from the wrong place. If the breach was a serious one you would be subject to disqualification unless you corrected the error.

o   If you elect to play your ball from G.U.R. and it does not clear the G.U.R. and becomes lost, you can drop a ball outside the G.U.R. without penalty. Alternatively you can, under penalty of one stroke, drop a ball in the G.U.R. as nearly as possible at the spot from which your original ball was last played.

o   If your ball is embedded in G.U.R. in a closely mown area through the green, you can drop your ball in the G.U.R. and then elect to play the ball as it lies or take relief from the G.U.R.

o   If you have lifted your ball because it was unplayable, then find that it was in G.U.R., you can take relief from the G.U.R. In match play, however, if you declared your ball unplayable and then, after your opponent had played his next stroke, you took relief from G.U.R. you would have conveyed incorrect information as to strokes taken.

12
OBSTRUCTIONS

o   An obstruction is movable if it may be moved without unreasonable effort, without unduly delaying play and without damaging course property.

o   An obstruction is anything artificial. The following are examples of movable obstructions which might be found on a golf course:-

- chocolate wrapper
- cigarette packet
- abandoned golf ball
- umbrella forgotten by a player playing in front
- plastic bag
- rake
- flagstick

o   If your ball rests against a plastic bag and it moves when the bag is removed, your ball must be replaced without penalty.

o   If your ball sits on a plastic bag through the green it can be marked then lifted, the bag removed, and then your ball dropped as near as possible to the spot directly under where it lay on the bag.

o   After the first stroke on the tee the tee markers become obstructions.

o   If your ball lies against a movable obstruction in a bunker or water hazard and a loose impediment lies on top of the obstruction in such a position that you could not move the obstruction without moving the loose impediment, you are entitled to move the obstruction and, if the impediment is accidentally moved in the process, you incur no penalty and you must place the loose

LOHIMP = loss of hole in match play
TSISP = two strokes in stroke play

impediment as nearly as possible at the spot where it originally lay.

o   If you take a practice swing in the rough and dislodge a concealed ball (an obstruction), there is no penalty since you did not play a practice stroke or a stroke with a wrong ball.

o   If your ball is lying on either a movable (rake) or immovable obstruction (rake holder) in a bunker, your ball is considered to be in the bunker, even though the margin of a bunker does not extend vertically upwards.

o   A stake supporting a young tree is not readily removable so it is an immovable obstruction and relief can be taken without penalty.

o   A bridge over a water hazard is an obstruction. You can ground your club, if your ball lies on it, at address or in the backward movement for the stroke.

o   If your ball comes to rest against a movable obstruction and you want relief you must move the obstruction. If you treat it as an immovable obstruction and you lift and drop your ball you incur a penalty of one stroke and you must replace your ball before playing your next stroke, otherwise the penalty is LOHIMP or TSISP.

o   If your ball comes to rest in a bunker against a movable obstruction – a rake – and the ball rolls away closer to the hole when the rake is removed, it must be replaced. If it will not stay due to a slope in the compacted sand and there is no other place not closer to the hole, you must drop your ball, under a penalty of one stroke, outside the bunker.

o   A log is a loose impediment until it is transformed into a bench which is an obstruction.

o   When a road is covered with gravel it becomes an artificially surfaced road and is thus an obstruction.

o   A stile attached to a boundary fence is an obstruction unless declared an integral part of the course.

o   If a part of the boundary fence is bowed towards the course so that it is inside the boundary line formed by the fence posts you cannot consider it to be an obstruction.

o   O.O.B. stakes between two adjacent holes, e.g. 2nd hole is O.O.B. when playing the 11th hole but 11th is not O.O.B. when playing the 2nd hole, may, by Local Rule, have been declared immovable obstructions when playing 2nd hole and fixed when playing the 11th hole. A line on the ground between the stakes is similarly defined. Check the scorecard.

o   If a stone has broken away from a retaining wall (immovable obstruction) in a hazard it becomes a movable obstruction which can be moved.

o   If your ball lies under a parked truck and the truck is movable you can treat it as a movable obstruction. If the truck is locked and not readily movable you can treat it as an immovable obstruction.

o   A road or path to which concrete, tar, gravel or wood chips have been applied is artificially surfaced and thus an obstruction.

o   Wood which has been manufactured into planks is an obstruction. This applies to wooden steps.

o   Turf raised by an underground pipe (obstruction) is not part of the obstruction.

o   If an opponent or fellow competitor removes a movable obstruction which you have asked not to be removed, the penalty is LOHIMP (opponent) or TSISP (fellow-competitor).

LOHIMP = loss of hole in match play
TSISP = two strokes in stroke play

o   An abandoned ball is a movable obstruction.

o   A movable artificial object lying O.O.B. can be moved if it interferes with your stance.

o   If your ball rests against a movable obstruction, don't hold the ball while you remove the obstruction. There is no penalty if your ball moves during removal of an obstruction, it is replaced. If you hold the ball you would incur a penalty stroke.

o   You cannot take relief from a sprinkler head if the interference is of a psychological nature. The sprinkler head must physically interfere with your stance or the area of your intended swing before you get relief.

o   When the position of a ball is such that there is interference by an immovable obstruction, there is a specific point on the course, not nearer the hole, nor on a putting green nor in a bunker or water hazard, nearest to which the ball originally lay at which, if the ball were so positioned, interference would cease to exist.

In determining the nearest point where interference would cease to exist, the club with which you would expect to play the next stroke MUST be used. In measuring one club length from the nearest point, you may use any club.

If the subsequent lie of the ball were such that it would be expedient for you to play your next stroke with some other club, you may do so.

o   If your ball is found in an immovable obstruction but not immediately recoverable you can substitute another ball and take relief without penalty.

o   If taking relief from an immovable obstruction incidentally gives relief from a boundary fence, you can take the relief.

LOHIMP = loss of hole in match play
TSISP = two strokes in stroke play

o   If taking relief from an immovable obstruction gives relief in your line of play, you do not have to drop so that your line of play is impeded.

o   If taking relief from an immovable obstruction in the rough, you can take the relief by dropping in the fairway if that is the nearest point.

o   If you take relief from one immovable obstruction and find that another immovable obstruction interferes with your swing, you are entitled to relief from the second obstruction.

o   You can take relief from an immovable obstruction in G.U.R. before deciding whether or not to take relief from the G.U.R.

o   Direction posts, which could interfere with the line of play, may have been declared as movable. Check the scorecard.

13
LOOSE IMPEDIMENTS

o   Loose impediments may be transformed into obstructions through processes of construction or manufacturing.   A log (loose impediment) which has been split and had legs attached has been changed by construction into a bench (obstruction).

A piece of coal (loose impediment) is an obstruction when manufactured into a charcoal briquette.

o   Examples of Loose Impediments are:

  −   stones
  −   leaves – when they don't adhere to your ball
  −   twigs – not fixed or growing
  −   pine needles
  −   branch – not fixed or growing
  −   dung
  −   worms
  −   worm casts
  −   insects
  −   ice
  −   fruit
  −   fruit skin (banana, orange)
  −   ant hill
  −   dead animal
  −   fallen tree not attached to the stump
  −   worm which is half underground and half above ground
  −   compacted soil aeration plugs (it is not loose soil)
  −   clod of earth (it is not loose soil)
  −   loose gravel on a road
  −   grass cuttings – when they don't adhere to the ball
  −   sand – on the green only
  −   loose soil – on the green only

LOHIMP = loss of hole in match play
TSISP = two strokes in stroke play

o Examples of items which are not Loose Impediments:

  – frost
  – dew
  – divot still partially attached to the ground
  – fallen tree attached to the stump
  – embedded acorn
  – loose soil from a removed molehill when it is not on the putting green

o Except on the line of putt, loose impediments can be removed by any means. On the line of putt you are restricted to removing loose impediments by picking them up or by brushing them aside.

o A stone of any size (not solidly embedded) can be removed, provided removal does not unduly delay play.

o If a stone is partially embedded and can be picked up with ease it is a loose impediment. When there is doubt as to whether it is solidly embedded or not, it should not be removed.

o Spectators, caddies, fellow competitors can assist in the removal of a large loose impediment.

o If part of a large branch which has fallen from a tree (thus a loose impediment) interferes with your swing you can break it off rather than move the whole branch.

o You can remove an insect which is on your ball through the green. It is not considered to be adhering to the ball and therefore is a loose impediment.

o Through the green you can remove loose impediments from the area in which you are preparing to drop your ball.

o   Before placing your ball (after dropping it twice) you can remove loose impediments on or around the spot on which the ball is to be placed.

o   If you have lifted your ball, to see if it is unfit for play, to identify it or because it interferes with another player's play, and a loose impediment which affected the lie has moved, you must replace the loose impediment before replacing your ball.

o   You can remove a loose impediment if it interferes with your stance even if it is lying O.O.B.

o   Even when your ball is not in a bunker or water hazard, but your opponent's or fellow competitor's is, don't remove a loose impediment in the bunker or water hazard which improves the lie of your opponent's or fellow competitor's ball. You would be penalised LOHIMP or TSISP.

o   If you accidentally kick a loose impediment (pine cone) into a bunker in which your ball lies, don't remove it, the penalty would be LOHIMP or TSISP.

o   If your ball comes to rest in front of a divot which is folded over but which is still attached to the ground you cannot remove it or replace it as it would improve the lie or the area of your intended swing. It is not a loose impediment. Penalty is LOHIMP or TSISP.

o   Don't replace a divot if your ball lies just in front of a divot hole. You may be guilty of improving the lie of the ball or the area of your intended swing. Replace the divot after you have played.

o   If you roll a large stone away from near your ball and press down some of the grass you are improving your lie or area of intended swing or your line of play. Penalty is LOHIMP or TSISP.

LOHIMP = loss of hole in match play
TSISP = two strokes in stroke play

o If you accidentally move a loose impediment in a bunker or water hazard there is no penalty as long as it was not moved in making the backswing and the lie of the ball or area of intended swing was not improved.

o In stroke play, if your ball moves when you remove a loose impediment in a bunker or water hazard you are penalised three strokes and the ball must be replaced. (Two strokes for moving a loose impediment and one stroke because the ball moved).

o In a bunker or water hazard, if you remove a loose impediment covering a ball which turns out not to be your ball, you are still penalised TSISP or LOHIMP.

o If your ball is in a water hazard and if you remove a loose impediment then decide not to play from the hazard, you are still penalised LOHIMP or TSISP.

o If your ball is in a bunker or a water hazard and your opponent, fellow competitor or partner plays a stroke and his divot comes to rest near your ball, you can remove the divot without penalty. You are entitled to the lie which your stroke gave you.

   The above would not be true if a natural object such as a pine cone landed near your ball. This is a natural cause, whereas the divot was caused by another player.

o If your clubhead touches a pine needle sticking up in the sand during your backswing in a bunker you are penalised LOHIMP or TSISP – it is a loose impediment.

o In a bunker covered in leaves you can remove as many leaves as will enable you to see part of your ball. If you touch the leaves (loose impediments) during your backswing you are penalised LOHIMP or TSISP.

o On the putting green you cannot remove loose impediments from your line of putt by brushing them aside with a cap or with a towel. You can only touch the line of putt in brushing them with your hand or a club.

o On the putting green you cannot remove loose impediments by vigorously sweeping them with the palm of your hand. Pick them up. Vigorous sweeping action exceeds that authorised.

o Try to remove loose impediments from your line of putt by brushing them aside. Minor brushing down the line of putt is allowed but it could be construed as influencing the movement of the ball when played.

o A dead animal is a loose impediment. A live one is an outside agency.

o In removing loose impediments from the vicinity of your ball, any accidental touching of the ball is not penalised provided the ball does not move, in which case there would be a one stroke penalty and the ball would have to be replaced.

o Don't place a fir cone or stick against your ball to prevent it from moving when you remove some loose impediments. Purposefully touching your ball in play is penalised one stroke.

o If you move the ball on the putting green with your foot when removing loose impediments you are penalised one stroke and the ball must be replaced. You incur no penalty on the putting green if your ball moves in the process of removing a loose impediment, i.e. directly attributable to removal of the loose impediment.

o On the putting green, if you remove an insect off the ball and cause the ball to move, there is no penalty and the ball must be replaced.

o   If, through the green, you remove loose impediments near your
    ball, then find you have to lift your ball due to interference with
    another player's play and it moves after you replace it (before you
    address it), there is no penalty. The ball must be played as it lies.
    The presumption that the removal of loose impediments caused
    the ball to move would not be valid.

o   Grass adhering to your ball is not a loose impediment and you
    cannot remove it.

o   Grass cuttings are loose impediments whether or not they have
    been piled for removal (G.U.R.), and you can remove them.

o   Pine needles piled for removal are loose impediments or G.U.R.

14
AN UNPLAYABLE LIE

o   You can deem your ball to be unplayable anywhere on the course except when your ball lies in or touches a water hazard. You can take relief under:

    a)   stroke and distance penalty

    b)   drop a ball within two club lengths of the spot where the ball lies unplayable

    c)   drop a ball behind the unplayable lie, keeping that point directly between the hole and the spot on which the ball is dropped (see Section 21).

o   If your ball is lodged high in a tree you can declare it unplayable and you can then shake the tree to dislodge the ball.

o   If your lie is changed by a tractor which creates a ridge near your ball, you can place your ball without penalty, in the nearest lie, within one club length, most similar to that which it originally occupied.

o   If your ball lies between two exposed tree roots and is clearly unplayable because of the roots, yet there is an immovable obstruction so located that it would interfere with your backswing, there is no relief from the obstruction. You must declare the ball unplayable.

o   If your ball is in a bunker completely filled with casual water one of the relief options is to declare your ball unplayable and play a ball as nearly as possible at the spot from which the original ball was last played.

LOHIMP = loss of hole in match play
TSISP = two strokes in stroke play

o   If your original ball may be lost in thick grass and you play a provisional ball, the provisional ball has to be abandoned if your original ball is found but is unplayable. You must continue with the original ball.

o   You can declare your ball unplayable without locating it and proceed under the stroke and distance penalty for relief. For relief which requires reference to where the ball lay, you must find and identify your ball.

o   If you declare your ball unplayable and drop your ball within two club lengths of the spot where it lay and it comes to rest in the same position, the ball is in play and must be declared unplayable again.

o   If you declare your ball unplayable through the green you can drop your ball in a bunker or water hazard when taking relief.

o   If, after your tee shot, you find your ball unplayable but the only relief option available is the stroke and distance penalty and you play it into another unplayable lie, the only relief option now open is to drop the ball two club lengths as many times as it takes to get the ball into a playable position.

   If as above you went back to the tee after your second shot you would be playing from the wrong place, the penalty for which is LOHIMP or disqualification.

o   If your tee shot finishes in tree roots and you play a stroke at it but miss, you cannot declare the ball unplayable and return to the tee. You have to play the ball from the spot from which the ball was last played, which was in the tree roots.

o   If your tee shot hits a rock and rebounds behind you into an unplayable lie, you can play again from the tee under the stroke and distance relief option.

o   If your ball is lying on grass-covered ground within a bunker and you declare it unplayable you may drop it outside the bunker. The grass-covered ground within a bunker is not part of the bunker.

o   If you declare your ball unplayable in a bunker you can only drop a ball outside the bunker by taking the stroke and distance relief option. Other relief options require the ball to be dropped in the bunker and if dropped outside you would be disqualified.

o   If you declare your ball unplayable eight feet off the ground up a tree you may obtain relief within two club lengths and drop a ball within two club lengths of a point on the ground under your ball. The position may be on the green.

   If your ball is at the bottom of a cliff you cannot proceed as in the case above. Your ball is now on the ground and the two club lengths must be measured from the point on the ground. The two club length relief option is not therefore available.

o   If you lift your ball because it was unplayable, then find you were in G.U.R., you may then obtain relief from the G.U.R.

o   If you find a stray ball which is unplayable and, thinking it is your ball, take the stroke and distance penalty for relief and play the stray ball, then find your original ball in a playable position, your original ball is lost and the stray ball is in play.

   In the above the other relief options cannot be invoked because you need to know the position of your ball. If you dropped the stray ball it would be a wrong ball. The penalty is LOHIMP or TSISP and in stroke play you would have to continue with the original ball.

15
CASUAL WATER

o If your ball lies against an immovable obstruction in casual water you can take relief from the immovable obstruction or from the casual water.

o Soft mushy earth is not casual water unless water is visible on the surface before or after you take your stance.

o If a pond or ditch has overflowed, the overflow is casual water.

o If your ball plugs in the rough and no casual water is visible on the surface but the pitch mark in which your ball came to rest was filled with water, then the ball is deemed to be in casual water.

o If you have to press down hard with one foot to cause water to appear around the sole of your shoe, it is not casual water.

o If there is no casual water visible on the green but it is evident when you walk beside your line of putt, you cannot claim casual water unless it is visible around your feet when you take your stance.

o If there is reasonable evidence that your ball came to rest in a large amount of casual water and it can only be retrieved with difficulty you may treat the ball as lost in casual water and abandon it.

o You are not entitled to relief from casual water on the green if your ball lies off the green.

o When the position of a ball is such that there is interference by casual water, there is a specific point on the course (not nearer the hole, nor on a putting green, nor in a bunker or water hazard) nearest to which the ball originally lay at which, if the ball were so positioned, interference would cease to exist. In determining the nearest point, the club with which you would expect to play the next stroke must be used. In measuring one club length from the nearest point, you can use any club.

o   If, in taking relief from one area of casual water, you drop your ball and it rolls such that there is interference from a second area of casual water you cannot re-drop your ball but you can take relief from the second area of casual water.

o   You may incidentally improve your line of play, e.g. avoid playing over a bunker or a tree, in obtaining relief from casual water. That is your good fortune.

o   In a bunker completely covered by casual water, the place providing "maximum available relief" is the spot which provides the most relief for lie and/or stance.

o   If you drop a ball in casual water in a bunker completely covered by water and it rolls from a spot with 1/4in depth of water to one with 1/2in depth of water, you can re-drop and if the ball rolls again it can be placed.

o   If your ball lies in a bunker completely covered by casual water you can:

(a)   play the ball as it lies

   either

(b)   drop the ball in the bunker without penalty at the nearest place, not nearer the hole, where the depth of casual water is least

LOHIMP = loss of hole in match play
TSISP = two strokes in stroke play

or

(c) drop the ball behind the bunker under penalty of one stroke, on the line from the hole to the point where the ball lay (see Section 21).

(d) declare the ball unplayable.

o If you decide to take relief from casual water in a bunker by dropping in the bunker, but find a bad lie, you cannot then decide to invoke the option of taking a penalty stroke and dropping outside the bunker. The choice is either/or.

o If the nearest point of relief from casual water on the green is off the green in the rough, then, if you take relief you must place the ball in the rough.

o If your ball lies in casual water within an area of G.U.R. you can take relief (a) from the casual water, drop the ball in the G.U.R. and then either play the ball as it lies or take relief from the G.U.R. (b) from the G.U.R. and then the casual water.

o Be sure you don't mistake casual water for a water hazard when the water hazard has overflowed. The Rules for relief are quite different – casual water is one club length, with the original ball, while a water hazard is as far as you wish, with a ball. If you follow the water hazard Rule you would drop in a wrong place – penalty LOHIMP or TSISP.

As above, but you do not retrieve the ball. Again a ball dropped under the water hazard Rule would be a wrong ball. Penalty is LOHIMP or TSISP. In stroke play you would be required to rectify the error.

o If there is casual water beyond an area of rough and your ball is driven into the area and cannot be found and it is not known from

LOHIMP = loss of hole in match play
TSISP = two strokes in stroke play

the evidence that the ball is in the rough or in the casual water, you must proceed as if the ball was lost in the rough.

LOHIMP = loss of hole in match play
TSISP = two strokes in stroke play

16
YOUR STANCE

o You can place a club on the ground parallel to the line of play to assist you in aligning your feet properly, but you must remove it before playing your stroke otherwise you would be penalised LOHIMP or TSISP.

o You cannot place your pipe beside your ball when playing a stroke. Penalty is LOHIMP or TSISP.

o "Fairly" taking your stance is intended to limit you to what is reasonably necessary to take a stance without unduly improving your lie, area of intended swing or line of play. You are not entitled to a normal stance or swing, you must accommodate the situation in which the ball is found and take a stance as normal as circumstances permit.

Actions which constitute fairly taking a stance are:

– backing into a branch or young sapling if that is the only way to take a stance, even if this causes the branch to move out of the way or the sapling to bend or break

– bending a branch of a tree with the hands in order to get under the tree to play a ball

Actions which do not constitute fairly taking a stance are:

– deliberately moving, bending or breaking branches with the hands to get them out of the way of the backswing or stroke.

– standing on a branch to prevent it interfering with the backswing or stroke

72

- hooking one branch on another or braiding two weeds for the same purpose

- bending with a hand a branch obscuring the ball after the stance has been taken

- bending an interfering branch with a leg in taking a stance when the stance could have been taken without bending the branch

o   You cannot carry a mat and stand on it on the teeing ground; you would be building a stance for which the penalty is LOHIMP or TSISP.

o   You cannot kneel on a towel to play a stroke under a tree; you would be building a stance for which the penalty is LOHIMP or TSISP.

o   You cannot knock down the side of a bunker with your foot in an effort to get both feet on the same level; you would be building a stance, the penalty for which is LOHIMP or TSISP.

o   You can take your stance inside a bunker when the ball is outside the bunker. You can also ground your club in the sand or touch the sand during the backswing. The club may only be grounded lightly.

o   If you take your stance and place the club head in front of the ball and, before grounding the club head behind the ball, the ball moves, you are penalised one stroke and the ball must be replaced. You are deemed to have addressed the ball when the club was grounded in front of the ball.

o   If, outside a bunker or water hazard, you took your stance and the ball moved before you addressed it, there is no penalty. If, however, you caused it to move you would be subject to a one stroke penalty and the ball must be replaced.

o   If you take your stance in a bunker or water hazard without a club and the ball moves, you are subject to a one stroke penalty and the ball must be replaced.

o   If your ball in a bunker moves while you are taking a stance there is no penalty unless your approach to the ball or the act of taking your stance caused the ball to move, in which case there is a one stroke penalty and the ball must be replaced.

o   Your club is considered grounded in long grass when the grass is compressed to a point where it will support the weight of the club.

o   If your ball is perched on a tuft of grass and in taking your stance you rest the club head on the tuft behind the ball, you have grounded the club and therefore have addressed the ball. If the ball then moves, you incur a penalty stroke and the ball must be replaced.

o   If when addressing a ball which is precariously balanced you realise it may move and you step away and start again but don't ground your club, but before you strike the ball it moves, you are penalised one stroke and the ball must be replaced.

o   If after addressing your ball, the ball moves and is stopped by the club head, you are penalised one stroke and the ball must be replaced.

o   In a bunker completely covered by casual water the place providing maximum available relief applies to stance and lie, it might be such that the ball will be in shallower water than your feet or vice versa.

17
YOUR STROKE

o   If your ball breaks as a result of a stroke, the stroke is cancelled and you can play a ball, without penalty, on a tee from within the teeing ground, or drop a ball through the green, or by placing a ball on the green.

o   If you make practice strokes with a putter off the green while waiting for other players to putt, the penalty is LOHIMP or TSISP.

o   If you make a proper stroke at a range ball which has been hit onto your fairway the penalty is LOHIMP or TSISP.

o   If you break a branch of a tree when making your backswing and discontinue the stroke the penalty is LOHIMP or TSISP, because the backward movement of the club was not the backward movement for a stroke.

o   If your swing is impeded by an O.O.B. stake which is an immovable obstruction (i.e. it denotes O.O.B. from the adjacent fairway) and you move the obstruction, the penalty is LOHIMP or TSISP for improving the area of your intended swing by moving anything fixed (which an immovable obstruction is).   Relief is obtainable from immovable obstructions.

o   You cannot move, bend or break a tree or fixed artificial object which is O.O.B. and interferes with your swing.   The penalty is LOHIMP or TSISP.

o   If a pitch mark made by the ball as a result of the previous stroke interferes with your backswing, you cannot step on it.   You would be improving the area of your intended swing.

o   If your ball comes to rest under a tree you cannot shake off any water before playing your next stroke. You would be improving the area of your intended swing.

o   If you break a branch in taking a practice swing then decide to play in another direction, you are still penalised LOHIMP or TSISP.

o   If you start your downswing and your clubhead is deflected or stopped by a branch of a tree you are deemed to have made a stroke.

o   If you voluntarily check your downswing so that you no longer have the intention of striking the ball, you have not made a stroke. If the club does move the ball, however, you are deemed to have made a stroke and the ball must be played as it lies.

o   If the clubhead disengages from the shaft during the backswing you cannot then make a stroke, which is the "forward movement of the club" – a shaft is not a club.

o   If the clubhead separates from the shaft on the downswing and you continue the downswing you have made a stroke.

o   If the clubhead separates from the shaft on the downswing and you stop the downswing, you have not made a stroke. If the clubhead moves the ball on the tee there is no penalty, when the ball is in play you would incur a one stroke penalty and the ball must be replaced.

o   If the shaft of your club breaks during the downswing and you continue the swing but miss the ball yet the clubhead falls and moves the ball, the stroke counts and the ball is played as it lies.

o   If, in disgust after missing a short putt you hole the ball with the grip end of your putter, you are penalised LOHIMP or TSISP.

LOHIMP = loss of hole in match play
TSISP = two strokes in stroke play

The ball must be struck at with the head of the club. In stroke play the stroke counts.

o   If you only have a backswing of half an inch because of an O.O.B. stake you cannot make a swing. Such a short distance would cause a push the penalty for which is LOHIMP or TSISP.

o   You can swing at a fence against which your ball rests in order to move the ball. You would be deemed to fairly strike at the ball.

o   You cannot hold the club behind the ball with one hand and then strike the shaft with the other hand in order to move the ball. You would be deemed to have pushed the ball.

o   You cannot use more than one club to move the ball (for instance, if it is lodged in a bush). The ball has to be struck at with the head of "the" club, which is singular.

o   If your partner aligns your putter and then moves away, it is in order. Assistance does not apply prior to making a stroke.

o   You can hold an umbrella over your head with one hand while putting with the other. You cannot accept protection from the elements from someone other than yourself, but you are not prohibited from protecting yourself.

o   Your partner or caddie cannot stand between you and the setting sun so that the sun glare is not in your face. The penalty would be LOHIMP or TSISP.

o   If you play a stroke into clay or muddy ground and the ball rises, falls and adheres to the club, you are deemed to have stopped the ball and the penalty is LOHIMP or TSISP and in stroke play the ball must be dropped as near as possible to the spot where the ball adhered to the club.

o   If you play a stroke out of wet sand or soil and the ball adheres to the face of the club, the ball should be dropped, without penalty, as near as possible to the spot where the club was when the ball stuck to it.

o   If your ball rebounds and hits the face of your club the penalty is LOHIMP or TSISP and the ball must be played as it lies.

o   If your ball starts to move during the backswing and you strike it while it is still moving, there is no penalty because the ball began to move after the start of the backswing. If you caused the ball to move, had addressed it or had removed a loose impediment within one club length, you incur a penalty stroke.

o   If you swing at and miss a wrong ball the penalty is LOHIMP or TSISP.

o   If your stroke at your ball dislodges an abandoned ball there is no penalty.

o   If you play a stroke at a broken abandoned ball it counts as a wrong ball; penalty is LOHIMP or TSISP.

o   If you accidentally move a ball on the tee when taking a practice swing it is not a stroke and no penalty is incurred.

o   If your ball is in play and you accidentally move it with a practice swing you have not made a stroke but you moved a ball in play and incur a penalty stroke and the ball must be replaced.

o   If you cannot play a right-handed stroke because of the proximity of a boundary fence, but an immovable obstruction interferes with the backswing of a left-handed stroke you can take relief. You can then use a normal right-handed swing for your next stroke and if then the obstruction interferes with the swing or stance you can take relief for a right-handed swing.

LOHIMP = loss of hole in match play
TSISP = two strokes in stroke play

o   If you can play a right-handed stroke but, by playing a left-handed stroke there would be interference from an immovable obstruction, you cannot decide to play a left-handed stroke and obtain relief.

o   If your ball comes to rest in or near to a bird's nest you can drop your ball at the nearest spot not nearer the hole which would allow you to make a stroke without damaging the nest.

LOHIMP = loss of hole in match play
TSISP = two strokes in stroke play

18
PITCH MARKS

o   If your ball bounces out of, then spins back into, its pitch mark, it is deemed to be embedded in that pitch mark.

o   When your ball is embedded you must not repair the pitch mark before dropping. If you were to do so you would be improving the area in which the ball was to be dropped. The penalty would be LOHIMP or TSISP.

o   If, when taking relief from casual water, your ball embeds on impact after dropping, you are entitled to lift and re-drop.

o   If your ball keeps embedding when dropped you are entitled under equity to place the ball as near as possible to the spot where it embedded when re-dropped, but not nearer the hole.

o   If you drop a ball and it rolls back into the pitch mark, it is deemed to be embedded and a re-drop is permitted.

o   If your ball is embedded in G.U.R. in a closely mown area through the green, you can drop your ball in the G.U.R. and then elect to play the ball as it lies or take relief from the G.U.R.

o   If your ball embeds in the grassy side of a fairway bunker, ensure that the area is closely mown before taking relief.

o   If you drive your ball straight into a bank which is in the fairway, i.e. the ball is never airborne, you are not entitled to relief since the ball would not be embedded in its own pitch mark.

o   You can mark and lift your ball on the fairway to determine if it is embedded. You must announce your intention in advance to a fellow competitor or an opponent. A ball so lifted cannot be cleaned unless it is deemed to be embedded.

19
LIFTING THE BALL

o   Before you lift your ball for any purpose it is advisable to mark it – if it is to be replaced, you must mark it.

o   When you lift your ball lawfully, you can tee it up on the teeing ground, drop it through the green, drop it in a bunker or water hazard or place it on the green.

o   If your ball comes to rest on the apron of the green and you mistakenly believe it is on the green and mark it and lift it, you incur a penalty of one stroke.

   If you clean the ball there is no additional penalty.

o   During a search for your ball, if your caddie finds a ball, lifts it for identification without your authority and identifies it as your ball you are penalised one stroke. An additional penalty stroke for failing to announce the intention to lift the ball for identification is not applicable.

o   Your caddie cannot declare your ball unplayable. If he lifts it before you have had an opportunity to inspect the lie you would be penalised one stroke and you would be obliged to replace the ball and then decide if it was unplayable.

o   If your ball is to be lifted it can be lifted by you, your partner or another person authorised by you. This overrides any other statements which require that you shall lift the ball.

o   If your ball is to be replaced it can be replaced by you or your partner, regardless of who lifted it, or by the person authorised by you to lift it.

o   If you pick up your ball without marking it, you incur a penalty stroke and you must replace the ball.

o   In match play, if you lift your opponent's ball without his authority, you are penalised one stroke.

o   In match play, if your opponent lifts your ball without your authority, he incurs one penalty stroke (not LOH). Therefore, don't lift the marker thinking you have won the hole or you are penalised one stroke and the marker must be replaced and you must hole out, otherwise you will lose the hole.

o   In stroke play, if a fellow competitor lifts your ball without your authority there is no penalty. You must replace the ball.

o   If you have marked your ball on the green and accidentally step on the marker and it moves, you are penalised one stroke and you must place your ball as near as possible to its original position but not nearer the hole.

o   If you have marked your ball on the green and use your putter to press the marker down and move the marker, there is no penalty since the marker was moved in the process of marking the position of the ball.

o   If your opponent's caddie accidentally kicks and moves your ball marker closer to the hole, your opponent incurs a one stroke penalty and the ball marker has to be replaced as near as possible to the spot where it lay.

o   If you mistakenly think you have won a hole and you pick up your ball marker you incur a one stroke penalty and the marker or ball must be replaced.

o   If you mark your ball on the green to let the following match through and your ball marker is removed you must replace your ball as near as possible to where it lay on the green.

LOHIMP = loss of hole in match play
TSISP = two strokes in stroke play

o   If play is suspended and your ball marker on the green is blown away, you must place your ball as near as possible to where it lay on the green.

o   If you think your ball marker may assist your opponent or fellow competitor in aligning his putt, you can move the marker to one side even if your opponent or fellow competitor requires you to leave it where it was.

o   You can mark the position of your ball with the toe of a club, although it is not advised.

o   In a match, if you mark and lift your ball near the hole and your opponent asks you to replace it before he putts, you do not have to comply with his request. Your opponent is not subject to any penalty for asking you to replace it.

o   If your caddie lifts your ball from a water hazard without your authority, you incur a one stroke penalty. You can either replace your ball or incur an additional one stroke penalty and drop outside the water hazard.

20
CLEANING THE BALL

o   You cannot, through the green, remove cut grass adhering to your ball – it is not a loose impediment when it is adhering to the ball.

o   If your caddie lifts a ball because it interferes with the play of another player, care must be taken not to clean it.

Throwing the ball to you could cause it to be cleaned and any doubt would be resolved against you.

o   You can clean your ball when you lift it:

–   on the green
–   taking relief – from an unplayable lie; when your ball is embedded

o   You cannot clean your ball when you lift it:

–   to determine if it is unfit for play
–   for identification
–   when it is interfering with or assisting play

If you clean it the penalty is one stroke.

o   If lime has been used to mark lines on the ground and a ball lands on the lime and some adheres to the ball, it cannot be removed.

21
DROPPING THE BALL

o   You are the only person who can drop your ball. If you allow your caddie or partner to drop your ball you incur a one stroke penalty.

o   To drop a ball you stand erect facing in any direction, hold the ball at shoulder height and arm's length, with the arm in any position from your front to your side, and drop it.

o   When the ball has to be dropped as near as possible to a specific point (one club length; two club lengths) it cannot be dropped nearer the hole than the specific point. If it is, it must be re-dropped without penalty.

o   If you drop a ball in an improper manner and the error is not corrected, you are penalised one stroke.

o   A ball dropped within two club lengths of the margin of a lateral water hazard may come to rest almost four club lengths from the hazard margin.

   A ball dropped within one club length of the nearest point of relief from an immovable obstruction may come to rest almost three club lengths from the nearest point of relief.

o   When dropping a ball to take relief from casual water, G.U.R., a hole made by a burrowing animal, a water hazard, a bunker or an unplayable lie and taking the relief option which requires you to keep a point (where the ball lay; where the ball last crossed the margin of the water hazard) directly between the hole and the spot on which the ball is to be dropped, you cannot stand on that line facing the hole and drop a ball with your arm out to the side; your arm must be facing directly forward.

o   The term "through the green" means that when you drop a ball to take relief from casual water in the rough you can drop it in the fairway and vice versa.

o   Through the green, if your ball is embedded in its own pitch mark in a closely mown area, it can be lifted, but you cannot repair the pitch mark before dropping the ball. You would be improving the area in which the ball was to be dropped, by pressing down an irregularity of the surface. The penalty is LOHIMP or TSISP.

o   If your dropped ball rolls back into its pitch mark where it was embedded, it can be re-dropped without penalty.

o   You must re-drop your ball, without penalty if:

   (i)   it touches you, your caddie, your equipment, your partner, his caddie or his equipment before or after the ball strikes a part of the course.

   (ii)   it rolls into a water hazard.

   (iii) it rolls into a bunker.

   (iv)   it rolls out of a water hazard.

   (v)   it rolls out of a bunker.

   (vi)   it rolls onto a putting green.

   (vii) it rolls O.O.B.

(viii) it rolls to a position where there is still interference from the immovable obstruction from which relief was being taken.

(ix) it rolls to a position where there is still interference from the G.U.R. or casual water from which relief was being taken.

(x)   it rolls and comes to rest more than two club lengths from where it first struck a part of the course.

(xi) it rolls and comes to rest nearer the hole than its original position.

If, after re-dropping, the ball rolls into positions (ii) to (xi) above, it has to be placed as near as possible to the spot where it first struck a part of the course when re-dropped.

o   Through the green you cannot remove or brush away sand or loose soil from the area in which you are preparing to drop a ball. Sand or loose soil are not loose impediments unless they are on the green.

o   If you mark the place where you can drop the ball with a golf glove and the ball strikes the glove, the ball must be re-dropped since the golf glove is equipment.

o   If you lift your ball when you are not entitled to do so and after learning of your error, you drop your ball rather than replace it, you incur a penalty of LOHIMP or TSISP.

o   When you drop a ball, check that it has been correctly dropped before picking it up and dropping again – this is particularly true of lateral water hazards. If, incorrectly believing the dropped ball had rolled too far, you lift it, you incur a penalty of LOHIMP or TSISP.

o   If you drop your ball and it is accidentally deflected by your opponent you can play it as it lies or re-drop it without penalty.

o   If you use your driver to measure the one or two club lengths when taking relief, you must use the driver again to measure that the ball hasn't rolled more than two club lengths. You cannot change to a putter.

o   If you put spin on the ball purposely when dropping it and don't correct your error you incur a one stroke penalty for dropping a ball in an improper manner.

o   If when obtaining relief from G.U.R. you drop a ball in an improper manner and in a wrong place (i.e. two club lengths rather than one) you must correct the errors before playing a stroke, without penalty. Otherwise you incur a three stroke penalty in stroke play or LOHIMP.

o   If you drop a ball in an improper manner and address it and it moves you incur a penalty stroke because the ball was in play, even if you correct the dropping error.

o   If you have to drop a ball and there is a branch in the way, you cannot have your caddie hold back the branch while you drop the ball.

o   If you drop a ball and it lodges in a bush, the ball is in play.

o   If you take relief from G.U.R. and you drop the ball and it rolls into a position where you would have to stand in G.U.R. to play a stroke, you must re-drop the ball.

o   If you drop a ball and it strikes a branch and bounces outside the area allowed, it is in play unless it rolls into a position which allows a re-drop (into a hazard, out of a hazard, onto a putting green, O.O.B., two club lengths or nearer the hole) and it must not be re-dropped. In measuring the two club lengths to determine if a re-drop is required the point on the ground immediately below the spot where the ball first struck the branch is used.

o   If you drop a ball twice because it rolls nearer to the hole and then drop it a third time rather than placing it and play it the penalty is LOHIMP or TSISP. If, before playing your ball, you lift it and place it where it first struck the course when re-dropped, there is no penalty.

o   Don't place a ball because you know, if it is dropped, that it will roll into a hazard or move more than two club lengths. Dropping and re-dropping are necessary to resolve any doubt and to establish the spot at which the ball must be placed, if necessary.

o   If you declare your ball unplayable and decide to drop it within two club lengths, you cannot change options if the ball rolls into a position which requires a re-drop.

o   If when measuring that your ball, after being dropped, has rolled more than two club lengths you accidentally move the ball, there is no penalty. If the ball had rolled more than two club lengths it must be re-dropped, if it had not rolled more than two club lengths it must be replaced.

o   If you drop a ball when you should have placed it or place it when you should have dropped it, before playing a stroke you may lift the ball, without penalty, and proceed correctly. If you don't the penalty is LOHIMP or TSISP.

o   If you declare your ball unplayable and decide to drop a ball behind the point where the ball lay and then drop your ball in a wrong place and lift it, you can then proceed to drop your ball within two club lengths.

LOHIMP = loss of hole in match play
TSISP = two strokes in stroke play

o   If, when taking relief from an obstruction, you mistakenly drop a ball other than the original ball, you must lift the dropped ball, which was substituted in error, without penalty, and drop the original ball.

o   It is permissible, through the green, to remove loose impediments from the area in which you are preparing to drop your ball.

o   When taking relief from casual water in a bunker the place providing "maximum available relief" might be such that the ball, when dropped, is in shallower water than your feet after you take your stance or vice versa.

o   When taking relief from casual water in a bunker if, having selected the place providing "maximum available relief" and dropping, your ball rolls into a place which does not give the maximum relief, you may re-drop. If it rolls again it may be placed where it first struck the bunker when re-dropped.

o   If your ball lies in casual water in a bunker and the maximum available relief is provided by a point at the edge of the bunker, you cannot drop outside the bunker and let the ball roll into it. The penalty, if you do and play the ball, is LOHIMP or TSISP.

o   If your ball lies in a bunker completely covered by casual water you may play the ball as it lies or:

(i)   drop the ball in the bunker without penalty at the nearest place, not nearer the hole, where the depth of casual water is least

or

(ii)   drop the ball behind the bunker under penalty of one stroke *or*

(iii) declare the ball unplayable.

o   If your ball lies in a bunker completely covered by casual water and you elect to drop the ball in the bunker but don't like the result, you cannot then invoke the option to take a penalty stroke and drop outside the bunker. The options are either/or.

o   If your ball is in casual water on the edge of a water hazard, make sure you proceed correctly. Taking relief as if the ball was in the water hazard would be penalised LOHIMP or TSISP.

When proceeding correctly, the ball which was played into the casual water should be retrieved if possible and dropped.

o   If you declare your ball unplayable and drop your ball in an area of G.U.R. from which play is prohibited, you must take the mandatory relief from the G.U.R.

o   If your ball lies in pine needles which are piled for removal, you may remove the pine needles (loose impediments) or drop away (G.U.R.).

o   If your ball lies behind a tree and a sideways stroke would be interfered with by a cast made by a burrowing animal, you may take relief and if the relief gets you out from behind the tree, you are entitled to play towards the green.

o   If your ball bounces out of its pitch mark and then spins back into it, you are entitled to drop it.

o   If you drop a ball on the fairway and the ball embeds on impact you may re-drop.

If when re-dropped the ball embeds, it may be placed as near as possible to the spot where it embedded when re-dropped but not nearer the hole.

o   If your ball is embedded in G.U.R. in a closely mown area through the green, you may drop a ball within the G.U.R. and then elect whether to play the ball as it lies or take relief from the G.U.R.

o   If you play a ball from within a water hazard into an O.O.B. area, you cannot place a ball from where you played (because if dropped it will roll into deep water). You can drop a ball under stroke and distance penalty or take the stroke and distance penalty and an additional penalty stroke and put a ball in play outside the hazard.

o   If your ball lies in a water hazard you can take relief by keeping the point at which the ball last crossed the margin of the water hazard directly between the hole and the spot on which the ball is dropped. The ball can then be dropped in a bunker or another water hazard.

o   If your ball crosses a water hazard and spins back into the water hazard, don't treat the water hazard as lateral and drop a ball across the water hazard within two club lengths of where it crossed the water hazard margin when it spun back into the water hazard. The penalty would be LOHIMP and disqualification in stroke play.

o   If you are unable to find your ball you cannot drop a ball in the vicinity of where it was lost. The penalty is LOHIMP. In stroke play you incurred a stroke and distance penalty plus an additional penalty of two strokes for playing from a wrong place. The breach was a serious one so you would be subject to disqualification unless you corrected your error.

LOHIMP = loss of hole in match play
TSISP = two strokes in stroke play

o   If you declare your ball unplayable and drop it and it comes to rest in its original position you must declare it unplayable again. Once dropped the ball is in play.

o   If you declare your ball unplayable through the green you can drop it in a bunker or water hazard.

22
ADVICE

o   Before starting your round you can ask a player who has completed his round what clubs he used at various holes.

o   You can seek advice from a fellow competitor after completing 18 holes of a 36 hole competition.

o   During a round you cannot tell an opponent or fellow competitor that he is over swinging, which club to use or the way to use it – that is advice.

o   Information as to the length of the hole is not advice. You can ask an opponent or fellow competitor for such information without penalty.

o   You can ask anyone to inform you as to the distance from a fixed object, e.g. a tree, bunker, to the centre of the green.

    You can only ask your partner or either of the caddies to inform you as to the distance from your ball to the green.

o   You can enquire as to the accuracy of the placement of 150 yard markers to the centre of the green.

o   You can enquire as to what club a player used at a previous hole.

o   Once you have played to the green, you can ask another player what club he took.

o   After playing a stroke you can only make a comment about wrong club choice if it does not influence another player's choice of club.

LOHIMP = loss of hole in match play
TSISP = two strokes in stroke play

o   After playing a stroke you cannot make a misleading comment about your club choice which you know will be overheard by an opponent or fellow competitor with a similar shot; the penalty is LOHIMP or TSISP.

o   You cannot suggest to your opponent or fellow competitor that he should declare his ball unplayable. The penalty is LOHIMP or TSISP.

23
LINE OF PLAY

o   Your "line of play" is the direction which you wish your ball to take after a stroke, plus a reasonable distance on either side of the intended direction. The line of play extends vertically upwards from the ground, but does not extend beyond the hole.

o   You can have the line of play indicated to you by anyone, but no one can stand on or close to the line of play while you play your stroke. Neither can you leave a mark which you make to indicate the line. The penalty would be LOHIMP or TSISP. The exception to this is that the flagstick can be held up to indicate the position of the hole before and during your stroke.

o   If you remove a post defining O.O.B. on your line of play you are penalised LOHIMP or TSISP even though you replace the post before playing a stroke.

o   You may determine if a long blade of grass, a twig or some similar natural object, which interferes with your swing, is loose or is attached to its roots, provided that, if the object is found not to be loose (i) it has not become detached and (ii) it is returned to its original position before the next stroke. If not the penalty is LOHIMP or TSISP.

o   If there is a bunker between your ball and the green you cannot smooth footprints in it since such action would improve the line of play. Penalty is LOHIMP or TSISP.

o   If there is a bunker between your ball and the green and you walk through it to remove a rake on your line of play, you cannot smooth the footprints you have made. You can worsen your line of play but you cannot then restore it to its original condition. The penalty is LOHIMP or TSISP.

o   If there is a bunker between your ball and the green you can test the condition of the bunker to determine whether it is feasible to putt through it. The prohibition on testing the condition of a bunker applies when your ball lies in or touches the bunker. However, if such testing improved the line of play the penalty is LOHIMP or TSISP.

o   If there is a bunker between your ball and the green and you decide to putt through it, you can remove a small stone (loose impediment) in the bunker on your line of play.

o   You cannot remove a stone from a stone wall on your line of play – the wall is an immovable obstruction and is fixed. The penalty is LOHIMP or TSISP.

o   Stakes supporting young trees are immovable obstructions and cannot be removed. The penalty is LOHIMP or TSISP.

o   Don't mop up casual water on the putting green between your ball, which lies off the green, and the hole. The penalty is LOHIMP or TSISP.

o   You cannot remove dew or frost from your line of play. You can remove dew or frost from the area behind or to the side of your ball. The removal of dew or frost which occurs incidentally to some other action, e.g. removing loose impediments, repairing ball marks, is permitted.

o   If a fellow competitor repairs spike marks on your line of play with your sanction you are both penalised two strokes.

o   You cannot remove moss or a creeper in a tree if its removal would improve your line of play. Penalty would be LOHIMP or TSISP.

LOHIMP = loss of hole in match play
TSISP = two strokes in stroke play

o   If you bend a shrub when taking a practice swing, thus improving the area of your intended swing, you are penalised LOHIMP or TSISP.

24
PROVISIONAL BALL

o   You can play a provisional ball for a ball which may be lost outside a water hazard or may be O.O.B. You have to declare it as such before playing it, by using the word "provisional", or it becomes the ball in play.

o   If after playing a provisional ball you play a wrong ball thinking it is your provisional ball, you are penalised LOHIMP or TSISP, even though your original ball may be found and the provisional ball abandoned.

o   If your provisional ball played from the tee strikes and moves the original ball, the original ball must be replaced.

o   If you play a provisional ball from the tee into the same area as your original ball and both balls have identical markings:

(i)   if one ball is found in a water hazard and the other is not found – the ball found is the provisional ball

(ii)   both balls are found in the water hazard – you must return to the tee and play another ball, playing three

(iii) if one ball is found in the water hazard and one in the rough – you must return to the tee and play another ball, playing three

(iv)   if one ball is found in bounds and one O.O.B. – the ball in bounds must be presumed to be the provisional ball

(v)   if both balls are found in bounds – one must be selected and treated as the provisional ball

LOHIMP = loss of hole in match play
TSISP = two strokes in stroke play

(vi) if both balls are found in bounds, but one ball is unplayable – the playable ball or the unplayable ball may be treated as the provisional ball

(vii) if both balls are found in bounds and both balls are unplayable – either ball may be treated as the provisional ball.

o   In stroke play if you are in doubt as to whether your drive might be O.O.B. and you play a provisional ball then you find your original ball but cannot determine whether it is O.O.B. or not, you can treat the provisional ball as a "second ball".

o   You cannot declare a second ball if you are going to play both:

(a)   a provisional ball in case the original ball is lost outside a water hazard or O.O.B.

and

(b)   the ball in play in case the original ball is unplayable or in a water hazard.

o   If your ball may be O.O.B. you must inform your opponent, marker or fellow competitor that you intend to play a provisional ball. If you don't it is the ball in play.

o   You cannot play a provisional ball if the original ball might be in a water hazard, but is clearly not lost outside the water hazard or O.O.B. If you play another ball it is the ball in play.

o   There must be a reasonable possibility that your ball is lost outside a water hazard or is O.O.B. before you can play a provisional ball. If there is no reasonable possibility, the second ball becomes the ball in play.

o   You can play a second provisional ball if you think the first one may be O.O.B. The second provisional ball bears to the first provisional ball the same relationship as the first provisional ball bears to the original ball.

o   If you prefer the position of a provisional ball you don't have to look for the original ball and if you play a stroke with the provisional ball from a position which is closer to the hole than where the original ball might be, that ball is the ball in play. This is true even if your opponent searches for the original ball and requires you to replay the stroke with the provisional ball because it was closer to the hole than his ball. The original ball is lost when you play a stroke out of turn with the provisional ball.

o   If at a par 3 your provisional ball goes in the hole, it becomes the ball in play when you pick it out of the hole unless your original ball has already been found in bounds within five minutes of your opponent or fellow competitor searching for it.

o   Your original ball becomes lost, even though it may be found, when the provisional ball is played from a position at or closer to the hole than where the original ball may be.

o   Once you have played a provisional ball from a position at or closer to the hole than where the original ball may be, the original ball is lost, even though it may subsequently be found much closer to the hole than that point.

    If you play the original ball you are playing a wrong ball since your original ball was deemed to be lost and therefore out of play. The penalty is LOHIMP or TSISP.

o   You can abandon your original ball after a short search and walk forward to play your provisional ball, but if the original ball is found by an opponent or fellow competitor within the five minute limit and before you play the provisional ball, it is in play and must be played.

o   If your original ball may be O.O.B. and you play a provisional ball into the same area and you think you have found your original ball but it is your provisional ball, and you play it, you have played a stroke with your provisional ball from the place where your original ball is likely to be and it is therefore in play and the original ball is lost.

o   Make sure your original ball is O.O.B. when you have played a provisional ball. If you lift the provisional ball thinking your original ball is in bounds, but it isn't, you have lifted the ball in play, the penalty for which is one stroke and the provisional ball must be replaced.

o   In stroke play, if you have played a provisional ball because your original ball might be lost, then find a ball which you believe is your original ball and pick up your provisional ball and play the found ball but if it is not your original ball which cannot subsequently be found, you are penalised two strokes for playing a wrong ball, one stroke for lifting the provisional ball (the ball in play) and stroke and distance penalty for losing the original ball. You would be required to replace and play the provisional ball.

o   You are not precluded from playing a provisional ball if your original ball may have come to rest in a water hazard, if the original ball may also either be O.O.B. or lost outside the water hazard. If the ball is found in the water hazard, the provisional ball must be abandoned.

o   Check carefully that your ball is O.O.B. before playing a provisional ball which is nearer the hole. If your ball is in bounds and you do so, the provisional ball is a wrong ball, the penalty is LOHIMP or TSISP and you would be required to continue with the original ball.

o   If both original ball and provisional ball go O.O.B., your next stroke from the tee is your fifth.

LOHIMP = loss of hole in match play
TSISP = two strokes in stroke play

25
LOST BALL

o   You can take up to five minutes to search for your ball. If it appears that the ball cannot immediately be found, invite the following match to play through.

o   Before starting a search for your ball announce to your partner, fellow competitor or opponent the colour and identifying mark of your ball.

o   If you think, but without reasonable evidence, that your ball is lost in G.U.R. and you drop and play a ball, then your original ball is found beyond the G.U.R. area, you have played a wrong ball. The penalty is LOHIMP or TSISP and you must hole out with the original ball.

o   If you play a stroke at a ball which is in G.U.R. and it remains in the G.U.R. but cannot be found:

   (a)   you can drop a ball outside the G.U.R., without penalty

   (b)   you can drop a ball as near as possible to the spot from which the original ball was played in the G.U.R., under penalty of one stroke.

o   In order to treat a ball as lost in a water hazard there must be reasonable evidence that it entered the water hazard. If such evidence does not exist the ball must be treated as a ball lost outside the water hazard.

o   If there is reasonable evidence that your ball came to rest in a water hazard but cannot be found, you can proceed as if the ball was in the water hazard. If you drop a ball and then your original is found outside the water hazard, the original ball must be abandoned.

LOHIMP = loss of hole in match play
TSISP = two strokes in stroke play

o   If you search for three minutes for your ball, find a ball, play it, then discover it was a wrong ball, you are allowed only two minutes to continue the search for your original ball.

o   If you search for your ball for three minutes, find it and leave the area to get a club then return but are unable to find the ball, you are only allowed a further two minutes to search.

o   If your original ball and a provisional ball are in long grass but not close together, you are allowed five minutes to search for each. If both balls are so close together that they can be searched for simultaneously then you are only allowed five minutes to search.

o   If you find your ball after a search of six minutes and play it you have played a ball which was out of play and therefore a wrong ball. The penalty is LOHIMP or TSISP and the error would have to be corrected before playing from the next tee, otherwise you would be disqualified.

o   If you play a second ball from the tee and do not announce it as a provisional ball, the original ball is lost and the second ball is in play. You can, however, search for the original ball but you must not unduly delay play.

o   If you and your fellow competitor/opponent are playing identical balls and they both land in the same area and therefore you could not determine which ball is which, they are both deemed lost.

o   If your original ball might be lost and you play a provisional ball into the same area and if the provisional ball and the original ball are identical and one ball is found in a water hazard and the other lost, the found ball is the provisional ball.

o   If your ball is lodged high in a tree but you cannot identify it as your ball, your ball is deemed to be lost.

LOHIMP = loss of hole in match play
TSISP = two strokes in stroke play

o   You cannot render a ball lost by declaration – the original ball is in play until another ball is put into play or a search time of five minutes has elapsed.

o   If you go back to the tee because your ball is not found, tee a ball but don't play it and your ball is then found within the five minute search period, you may play the original ball. The teed ball was not in play since you had not made a stroke at it.

If, as above, you go back to where your second shot was played and drop a ball, that ball is in play and the original ball was lost, even though it had been found within the five minute search period.

o   If you believe you are unable to find your ball because it has been moved by an outside agency, although there is no definite evidence of such, and you drop a ball where you think your original ball came to rest, you dropped a ball in the wrong place. The penalty is LOHIMP. In stroke play you incurred a stroke and distance penalty plus an additional penalty of two strokes for playing from a wrong place. The breach was a serious one so you would be subject to disqualification unless you corrected your error.

o   If you are unable to find your ball and you drop another ball in the area where the original ball was lost and play it, you played from the wrong place, the penalty is LOHIMP. In stroke play you incurred a stroke and distance penalty plus an additional penalty of two strokes for playing from a wrong place. The breach was a serious one so you would be subject to disqualification unless you corrected your error.

o   A provisional ball which has been holed becomes the ball in play as soon as you pick it out of the hole, provided the original ball has not already been found in bounds within five minutes of an opponent or fellow competitor looking for it.

LOHIMP = loss of hole in match play
TSISP = two strokes in stroke play

o   If your original ball might be lost and you play a provisional ball adjacent to the hole, you can decide not to look for your original ball. However, if a member of the Committee, a forecaddie, your opponent or a fellow competitor finds your original ball even though you decline to search for it, you must inspect the ball and if it is your original ball, you must continue to play with it.

26
PLAYING A WRONG BALL

o   There is no penalty if you play a wrong ball out of a bunker or water hazard. You have then to play your ball.

o   If you swing at and miss a wrong ball the penalty is LOHIMP or TSISP.

o   If you play a stroke at your ball in the rough and also hit an abandoned ball which was hidden beneath your ball there is no penalty since you did not play a stroke with the hidden ball. You must play your ball as it lies.

o   If you play a stroke at part of a broken ball thinking it is your ball it is a wrong ball and the penalty is LOHIMP or TSISP.

o   If you mark your ball on the green and set it aside but, by mistake putt it from the place it was set aside you are playing a ball which is not in play and is therefore a wrong ball. Penalty is LOHIMP. Penalty in stroke play is TSISP and you are required to correct the error before playing from the next tee otherwise you would be disqualified.

o   If you play another ball when yours is not found after a brief search it becomes the ball in play. Even if your original ball is found within the five minute limit it is a lost ball. If you lift the second ball and play your original ball you are playing a wrong ball. When you lifted the second ball you were penalised one stroke. You also incur LOHIMP or TSISP and you must rectify the error or you would be disqualified.

o   If you play a ball which is out of bounds it is a ball which is not in play and therefore a wrong ball. Penalty is LOHIMP or TSISP and you must then add the stroke and distance penalty.

LOHIMP = loss of hole in match play
TSISP = two strokes in stroke play

o   If you realise that you and your opponent or fellow competitor are playing identical balls, don't substitute another ball during the play of a hole, it would be a wrong ball. The penalty would be LOHIMP or TSISP and you would also be penalised one stroke for lifting your ball without authority.

o   If your ball is lost in G.U.R. and you treat it as a lost ball and take the stroke and distance penalty and play another ball, that is the ball in play. If you then realise that you are entitled to G.U.R. relief without penalty and you abandon the ball played as a lost ball and drop another ball under G.U.R. relief and play it, the penalty would be LOHIMP. In stroke play you incur the stroke and distance penalty plus a penalty of two strokes for lifting a ball in play and failing to replace it, and you must correct your error or be disqualified. You incur an additional penalty of two strokes for wrongly substituting a ball.

o   If you hit a wrong ball out of bounds and play another ball under stroke and distance penalty, then discover your original ball in bounds, the penalty is LOHIMP or TSISP and you must continue play with your original ball; the ball played under stroke and distance penalty is a continuation of the play of the wrong ball.

o   If you find a ball O.O.B. and, thinking it is your ball, play it from the spot from which your original ball was played, then find your original ball in bounds, the original ball is lost and the ball found O.O.B. is in play under penalty of stroke and distance. It is not a wrong ball.

o   If you find a ball which you declare is unplayable and drop it, then find it is not your ball, there is no penalty. There is no penalty for lifting and dropping a wrong ball. The penalty is for playing a wrong ball. You can continue the search for your original ball.

o   There is no penalty for playing a wrong ball out of a bunker even if you have declared it unplayable in the bunker and lifted and dropped it.

108

LOHIMP = loss of hole in match play
TSISP = two strokes in stroke play

o   If you marked and lifted your ball on the green and threw it to your caddie for cleaning and he missed it and it went into a lake from which it was not recoverable, you would have to hole out with another ball and the penalty is LOHIMP or TSISP.

o   If you mark and lift your ball on the green and by mistake place another ball on the spot from which your original ball was lifted, then discover the error and re-mark, lift and then replace the original ball, there is no penalty since you did not play a stroke with the other ball.

     If you mark and lift your ball on the green and by mistake place another ball on the spot from which your original ball was lifted and play it the penalty is LOHIMP or TSISP.

o   In stroke play, your fellow competitor marked the position of your ball on the green, lifted it and placed it nearby on the green. You putted it from where it lay and holed out.

     When the ball was lifted, it was out of play. When you played a stroke at it, it was a wrong ball.

     If you knew your fellow competitor had lifted your ball you would be penalised two strokes and the ball must be replaced on the correct spot.

     If you did not know that your fellow competitor had lifted your ball there is no penalty and the ball must be replaced where it was marked.

     If you learned of the mistake after playing from the next tee, your score with the wrong ball would stand without penalty.

o   In a match if you concede the hole, then your opponent discovers that he has played a wrong ball, you won the hole before you conceded it.

o   In a match if your opponent won the hole then, after driving from the next tee it was discovered that your opponent had played a wrong ball, you can claim the hole since your opponent had failed to inform you promptly that he had incurred a penalty for playing a wrong ball.

o   In match play, if your opponent plays a wrong ball from a bunker and it knocks your ball into the hole, there is no penalty and you must replace your ball.

o   If your ball is in casual water and you mistake it for the adjacent water hazard and you don't retrieve your ball but drop another ball 10 yards behind the casual water as if it had been in the water hazard, the ball substituted was a wrong ball. The penalty is LOHIMP or TSISP and in stroke play you are required to proceed as if your ball had been lost in casual water.

o   If you consider that your ball is lost in G.U.R. and drop a ball outside the G.U.R. and play it, then find your ball beyond the G.U.R., you have played a wrong ball. The penalty is LOHIMP or TSISP and you must hole out with your original ball.

o   In stroke play, if you believe your original ball might be lost and play a provisional ball, then you find a ball which you believe to be your original ball and play it, pick up the provisional ball and then discover that the ball you played was a wrong ball. The original ball cannot be found so the provisional ball was the ball in play. The total penalty is five strokes, the stroke and distance penalty for a lost ball, a two stroke penalty for playing a wrong ball and a one stroke penalty for picking up the provisional ball. You were required to replace and play out with the provisional ball.

o   If you play a provisional ball from a place closer to the hole than your original ball which you think is O.O.B. but is not, you are playing a wrong ball. Penalty is LOHIMP or TSISP and you must hole out with your original ball. You must ascertain the status of

LOHIMP = loss of hole in match play
TSISP = two strokes in stroke play

your original ball before playing a provisional ball from a position closer to the hole.

o   If you find a stray ball in a bad lie and declare it unplayable and drop it within two club lengths of the spot where it lay and play it, then find your original ball in a playable position, you played a wrong ball. The penalty is LOHIMP or TSISP and you must hole out with your original ball.

LOHIMP = loss of hole in match play
TSISP = two strokes in stroke play

27
PLAYING FROM THE WRONG PLACE

o   If your tee shot, while still in motion, is deflected O.O.B. by a tractor you are required to treat the ball as O.O.B. thus incurring a stroke and distance penalty. If you drop a ball where the ball was deflected and play it, you are playing from a wrong place. Penalty is LOHIMP. In stroke play you would incur a penalty of stroke and distance for a ball O.O.B and an additional two strokes for a breach of the O.O.B Rule and, since the breach was a serious one, disqualification, unless you corrected the error.

o   If you declare your ball unplayable in a water hazard and drop the ball in the water hazard and play it, you are playing from a wrong place since a ball can't be declared unplayable in a water hazard. Penalty is LOHIMP or three strokes in stroke play and you must play out the hole with the ball so played.

o   If you inadvertently replace your ball on the green in a wrong place nearby and hole out you are penalised LOHIMP or TSISP.

In stroke play, if you discover the error and put the ball in the correct place and hole out there is no additional penalty; the ball played from the wrong place was in play and the hole was completed.

o   If you inadvertently replace your ball on the green in a wrong place, play it to a place near the hole, then discover your error and lift the ball and play it from the correct place, you are penalised LOHIMP or TSISP for playing from a wrong place and, in stroke play, a further two strokes for lifting the ball giving a total of four strokes.

o   If you believe your ball came to rest in a bunker but couldn't find it and you drop a ball in the bunker and play it to the green, beyond which your ball is subsequently found, you would be disqualified for playing from a wrong place well in advance of the spot from which your ball was last played, unless you rectified the error, in which case you would incur an additional penalty of two strokes.

o   If you accidentally step on your ball in the rough during a search you incur a penalty stroke and the ball must be replaced. If the original spot has been altered you can place the ball within one club length. If you place the ball outside the one club length the penalty is LOHIMP or TSISP.

As above except that instead of placing the ball you drop it. The penalty is LOHIMP or TSISP in addition to the one stroke penalty.

o   In stroke play if your ball in a bunker was played by a fellow competitor and he failed to get the ball out of the bunker but then found that he had played your ball and you play from the place to which the ball was played by your fellow competitor, the penalty is two strokes. You should have replaced your ball on its original lie in the bunker.

As above but your fellow competitor played the ball out of the bunker and you played it. You would be disqualified unless you rectified the error.

o   If your ball is in casual water and you mistake the casual water for the adjacent water hazard and proceed as if the ball had been in the water hazard and drop your ball 10 yards behind the casual water and play it, you have dropped the ball in the wrong place. Penalty is LOHIMP or TSISP.

28
INTERFERENCE

o   You can have another ball lifted if the ball interferes either physically or psychologically with your play.

o   You can request an opponent or fellow competitor to lift his ball if it is a few feet from the green on a direct line to the hole with your ball which is, say, 30 yards away.

o   If your ball is on the green it is not reasonable for an opponent or fellow competitor who has a full iron shot to the green to request that you mark and lift your ball because it interferes with his stroke.

o   If your ball is accidentally moved as you approach it to mark and lift it when it interferes with another player's stroke, there is a one stroke penalty and the ball must be replaced. If the ball is accidentally moved in the specific act of marking the position of or lifting the ball there is no penalty.

o   If you mark and lift your ball in match play, you do not have to replace it if your opponent requests you to do so.

o   In stroke play, a player off the green cannot request you to leave your ball on the green if it might act as a backstop. If you comply with such a request you would be agreeing to assist another player and both should be disqualified.

o   If your ball is in a position to assist the play of a fellow competitor you must mark and lift it. If you fail to take action to invoke the interference Rule it would be taken as evidence of an agreement to assist another player, the penalty for which is disqualification.

29
BALL MOVED

o   Your ball has moved horizontally or vertically when it does not return to its original position.

o   On the green if you rotate your ball to align the maker's name with the line without marking it, you incur a penalty stroke. There is no penalty if the ball is first marked.

o   If when addressing your ball you accidentally cause it to oscillate but it returns to its original position, then the ball has not moved.

o   If you take your stance and place the club head on the ground in front of the ball without pressing anything down and, before you ground the club behind the ball, the ball moves, you incur a one stroke penalty and the ball must be replaced. Placing the clubhead in front of the ball is deemed to be addressing it.

o   If you lift your ball on the putting green then accidentally drop it on another player's ball which is at rest, in match play you would incur a penalty stroke and your opponent must replace his ball; in stroke play there is no penalty and your fellow-competitor must replace his ball.

   A ball which has been lifted and not put back into play is equipment.

o   If your ball is at rest on the edge of a bunker and it falls into the bunker as you approach it, if there is evidence that you caused it to move it must be replaced and you incur a penalty of one stroke; if there is no evidence that you caused it to move then it is played as it lies.

o   If your ball on the green is moved by a ball played from an adjacent fairway it must be replaced. The other ball is an outside agency. If the ball is played from its new position the penalty is LOHIMP or TSISP.

o To treat a ball which cannot be found as moved by an outside agency rather than lost, there must be reasonable evidence to that effect.

o If your ball comes to rest in a plastic bag that has blown onto a fairway and the ball is moved as the bag is blown by the wind, the bag can be treated as an outside agency and you can drop the ball where it originally lay in the bag.

o If your ball is moved by your opponent dislodging a large stone when playing his stroke, the stone is an outside agency and your ball must be replaced. There are no penalties.

o If you replace your ball on the putting green and, before you address the ball it moves due to a gust of wind, you must play the ball from its new position. Wind is not an outside agency.

o If, playing from the teeing ground, you miss the ball completely, you cannot re-set the tee position. The penalty would be one stroke and the tee must be returned to its original position. The ball was in play once you made a stroke at it. If you played a stroke at the ball from the new tee position the penalty would be LOHIMP or TSISP.

o If, when starting a hole, you just dislodge the ball in making a stroke and you re-tee it, you incur a penalty stroke. If you then play the hole, the penalty is LOHIMP or TSISP.

o If you mistake an O.O.B. stake to be an obstruction and lift your ball and drop it, you incur a one stroke penalty and the ball must be replaced. If you play the ball the penalty is LOHIMP or a total of TSISP.

o   If you drop your ball away from a movable obstruction rather than moving the obstruction, you incur a one stroke penalty and the ball must be replaced. If you play the ball you incur a penalty of LOHIMP or a total of TSISP.

o   If your ball is lying on the putting green and it oscillates due to the wind, don't press it down into the surface of the green to stop it oscillating. You would incur a penalty stroke and since the original lie of the ball was altered when the ball was pressed down you would have to find a spot similar to the original lie to replace your ball. If you played a stroke from the pressed down position the penalty would be LOHIMP or a total of TSISP.

o   If your ball is moved by wind it must be played as it lies. If you replace it and play it you incur a penalty of LOHIMP or a total of TSISP.

o   If you play out of G.U.R. without realising it was G.U.R. then find out it was G.U.R., don't pick up your ball and proceed under the G.U.R. Rule. When you played from the G.U.R. the ball was in play. If you pick up a ball in play you incur a one stroke penalty and if you then play it a penalty of LOHIMP or a total of TSISP.

o   If you lift your ball without being entitled to and drop it rather than replace it you incur a penalty of LOHIMP or a total of TSISP.

o   If you hit a ball into a practice area which you think is O.O.B. but it isn't, and you lift it and replay it, you are subject to LOHIMP or a total of TSISP.

o   If you elect to take relief from G.U.R. then find that you can only drop the ball into an area which would make the ball unplayable, you cannot replace the ball in the G.U.R. without incurring a one stroke penalty.

o   If you mistakenly believe your ball is on the green when it is still on the apron and you mark, lift it and clean it, you incur a penalty stroke for lifting it but no penalty for cleaning it.

o   If, during a search for your ball your caddie lifts your ball for identification purposes without announcing his intention, you incur a one stroke penalty.

o   If your caddie considers your ball to be unplayable and lifts it you incur a penalty of one stroke. The ball must be replaced before you decide whether or not it is unplayable.

o   If you mistake your ball lying in the rough to be a wrong ball and ask a fellow competitor to pick it up, then find it was your ball in play, you incur a penalty stroke and the ball must be replaced.

o   If you drop a towel onto the ground and the wind blows the towel onto your ball and moves it, you incur a penalty of one stroke and the ball must be replaced. The towel is equipment.

o   In match play if you concede your opponent's next stroke and knock the ball away and it strikes and moves your ball, you incur a penalty of one stroke and you must replace your ball.

o   If you accidentally move your ball on the tee while taking a practice swing there is no penalty and the ball can be re-teed anywhere within the teeing ground.

o   If you accidentally move your ball when it is in play while taking a practice swing you incur a penalty stroke and the ball must be replaced.

o   If you play a wrong ball in a bunker and in so doing you move a nearby ball which turns out to be your ball you incur a one stroke penalty and your ball must be replaced. You could have had the ball marked and lifted. If the lie has been altered it should be recreated. There is no penalty for playing the wrong ball.

o   If you step on your ball in the rough and push it into the ground you incur a penalty of one stroke. Because the original lie has been altered you then have to place your ball in the nearest lie most similar to the original lie less than one club length away without penalty. If you place the ball more than one club length the penalty is LOHIMP or TSISP.

o   If you move your ball in the rough and the spot from which it moved is not determinable, you incur a one stroke penalty and you must drop your ball as near as possible to the place where it lay. If you place the ball the penalty is LOHIMP or a total of TSISP.

o   If you miss a shot completely but, in swinging the club back you accidentally knock the ball backwards, you incur a one stroke penalty and the ball must be replaced.

o   If your ball in stroke play stops on the lip of the hole and in disgust you knock the ball off the green, you incur a penalty of one stroke and the ball must be replaced. You are not considered to have made a stroke.

o   If you accidentally drop the flagstick and it moves your ball you incur a penalty of one stroke and the ball must be replaced, unless you were using the flagstick for measuring.

o   If your ball is lodged in a tree and you climb the tree to play it and dislodge the ball you incur a penalty of one stroke and the ball must be replaced.

o   If your ball is lodged high in a tree and you wish to declare it unplayable, you may dislodge it by shaking the tree so that you can identify it. You should state your intentions first.

o   If your ball is lost in a tree and you shake the tree and dislodge it, you incur a penalty stroke for moving the ball. The ball must be replaced. If you play it from where it fell the penalty is LOHIMP or a total of TSISP.

119

o   If your ball is lost in a tree and you shake the tree and dislodge it you incur a penalty of one stroke and the ball must be replaced.

   If the spot where it lay in the tree is not determinable you must place the ball as near as possible to the spot from which it moved.

   If the ball fails to remain on the correct spot when replaced you must place the ball as near as possible to the spot from which it moved.

   If you cannot reach the spot where the ball lay you must declare the ball unplayable, incurring an additional penalty stroke.

o   If your ball is lying in light rough and you take several practice swings near to it (one foot or so) and then take your stance but don't ground the club but the ball moves, there is evidence that you caused it to move and you would incur a penalty of one stroke and the ball must be replaced.

o   If your ball moves after you have taken your stance but before you have grounded your club there is no penalty. If, however, you caused the ball to move, the penalty is one stroke and the ball must be replaced.

o   If you enter a bunker or water hazard without a club and position your feet for determining how to play the stroke, you have taken your stance. If the ball then moves you incur a penalty of one stroke and the ball must be replaced.

o   If your ball moves in a bunker or water hazard while you are taking your stance there is no penalty. If, however, your approach to the ball or the act of taking your stance caused the ball to move then you incur a penalty stroke and the ball must be replaced.

o   If you ground your club with feet together when taking your stance before widening your feet to shoulder width, and the ball moves before you have completed your stance there is a penalty because you would be deemed to have moved the ball.

o   If your ball is perched on a tuft (grass, heather) and you take your stance and rest your club on the tuft and the ball moves, you have grounded your club and therefore have addressed the ball. There is a penalty of one stroke and the ball must be replaced.

o   If you take your stance and ground the club then realise that the ball is precariously balanced and move away, then retake your stance but do not ground your club and the ball moves, you incur a one stroke penalty and the ball must be replaced.

o   If your ball is lying on a slope and when you address it it moves and comes to rest O.O.B., there is a one stroke penalty and the ball must be replaced.

o   If your ball is on the edge of the hole and overhanging it and you address it and it falls into the hole, you incur a penalty of one stroke and the ball must be replaced.

o   If, after you have addressed your ball, a ball played from elsewhere strikes and moves your ball, it must be replaced, without penalty.

o   If, after you have addressed your ball, it moves and comes to rest against your club you incur a penalty stroke and the ball must be replaced.

o   If, in the process of removing a loose impediment on the green you accidentally move the ball with your foot, you incur a penalty stroke and the ball must be replaced.

o   If after addressing your ball on the green, an insect alights on your ball and you move the ball in attempting to brush the insect off the ball, there is no penalty and the ball must be replaced – the insect is a loose impediment.

o   In match play if your opponent, even though he has the right to require you to mark and lift your ball because it is lying close to his ball, plays and moves your ball, he incurs a penalty of one stroke and your ball must be replaced. If the lie of your ball has been altered you must place your ball in a lie similar to the original within one club length.

o   In match play, if your opponent disturbs some bushes in playing a stroke and causes your ball to move, your opponent incurs a penalty stroke and your ball must be replaced.

o   In match play, if your opponent's caddie accidentally steps on your ball, your opponent incurs a penalty stroke, unless the caddie was searching for the ball, in which case there would be no penalty.

o   In match play, if you find a ball and claim it as yours, then your opponent's caddie finds another ball and lifts it and it is subsequently discovered that the ball was yours there is no penalty and your ball must be replaced.

o   If your provisional ball from the tee strikes and moves your original ball there is no penalty and the original ball must be replaced.

o   If your ball is deflected by a direction post it is "rub of the green" and the ball must be played as it lies.

o   If you hit your ball onto another fairway and while it is still moving a player on that fairway hits it while making a stroke at his ball, you must play your ball as it lies. If it cannot be found you must treat it as a lost ball.

o   In a bunker, if the ball after a stroke rolls back and stops against your foot and moves when you move your foot, the penalty is LOHIMP or TSISP and in stroke play you must replace the ball on the spot at which it came to rest against your foot.

LOHIMP = loss of hole in match play
TSISP = two strokes in stroke play

o   If your ball lies on a slope through the green and you take a stance but do not ground your club because you fear the ball might move and the ball rolls backwards and is stopped accidentally by your club then rolls further down the slope when your club is removed, you are subject to a penalty of one stroke and the ball must be replaced where it came to rest against your club.

o   In stroke play, if your fellow competitor plays your ball and in so doing removes a divot, you can place your ball in the nearest lie most similar to the original lie within one club length.

o   If you accidentally drop a coin or a ball marker and it strikes and moves your ball on the green, you are penalised one stroke and the ball must be replaced.

30
ARTIFICIAL DEVICES

o   You cannot attach a distance meter to your golf cart for the purpose of measuring the distance of shots. Penalty would be disqualification.

o   You can gauge distance to the putting green by holding a scorecard or pencil at arm's length and comparing it with the height of the flagstick, provided that the scorecard or pencil had not been specially marked.

o   You can use standard spectacles or field glasses which have no range-finder attachments.

o   You cannot use a compass during a round to assist you in determining wind direction or the direction of the grain in the greens. Penalty would be disqualification.

o   You can use a booklet which contains illustrations of the holes on a course and determine the distance of your ball from the green.

o   You cannot hold a golf ball in your upper hand against the grip of your putter to assist in putting. Penalty would be disqualification.

o   You can apply adhesive tape to your fingers unless its use is to bind two fingers together to aid you in gripping the club.

o   You cannot use, during a round, a training club (e.g. one which emits a click if a practice swing is correctly timed; one with a weighted head cover). Penalty would be disqualification.

o   You cannot use a plumb-line to measure the slope of a green. Penalty would be disqualification.

LOHIMP = loss of hole in match play
TSISP = two strokes in stroke play

o   You can use your putter as a plumb-line to measure the slope of a green.

o   You can use a hand warmer, but you cannot use a ball warmer. Penalty would be disqualification.

LOHIMP = loss of hole in match play
TSISP = two strokes in stroke play

31
AN OUTSIDE AGENCY

o An "outside agency" is any agency not part of the match or, in stroke play, not part of the competitor's side, and includes a referee, a marker, an observer or a forecaddie. Neither wind nor water is an outside agency.

o If you have putted on the green and your ball strikes the hole-liner which has come out of the hole with the flagstick, if the hole-liner was moving when the ball struck it, the stroke is cancelled and the ball must be replaced. If the hole-liner was not moving, the ball must be played as it lies. In case of doubt the ball must be played as it lies. The hole-liner is an outside agency.

o A live animal is an outside agency. A dead one is a loose impediment.

o In order to treat a ball which cannot be found as moved by an outside agency rather than lost, there must be reasonable evidence to that effect.

o If you are unaware when you play your ball that it had been moved by an outside agency, then subsequently learn that it was, there is no penalty.

o If your ball is moved by an outside agency and because the area is not visible because of a hump, for example, you should drop your ball in an area which is neither the most, nor the least favourable of the areas where your ball might have been.

o If your ball comes to rest inside a plastic bag and it moves due to a gust of wind, the bag should be treated as an outside agency and you should drop the ball directly under the place where it originally lay in the bag.

o   If your ball is moved by a stone which is dislodged by another player's stroke your ball must be replaced. The stone was an outside agency.

o   If you ask a spectator to attend the flagstick and he kicks your ball away when it finishes close to the hole, there is no penalty and you must replace your ball and hole out with it. The spectator was an outside agency.

o   While play was suspended, wind or casual water moves your ball. Neither of these is an outside agency but your ball should be replaced, if the place was not determinable then the ball should be dropped as near as possible to the place where it lay. When play was suspended it has to be resumed from where it was discontinued.

o   If you miss-hit your ball onto another fairway and it is struck by another player in the course of him taking his stroke and cannot be found, you must treat the ball as lost. The other player was an outside agency. If your ball had been found you would have had to play it from where it came to rest.

o   If, on the green, your ball is deflected into the hole by a moving outside agency you must replay the stroke. If you do not replay the stroke, in stroke play you would be disqualified.

o   If your ball is still in motion on the green having been played from off the green and it is moved by a dog, if it was deflected it should be played as it lies without penalty; if it was picked up it should be placed, without penalty, as near as possible to the spot where the original ball was when the dog picked it up.

o   If your ball in motion, on the green, is deflected or picked up, the stroke is cancelled and the ball must be replaced.

o   If you play a stroke on the green and while your ball is in motion a ball played at another hole strikes your ball, the stroke is cancelled and you must replace your ball. The other ball is a moving outside agency.

o If you are unable to find your ball and believe, without reasonable evidence, that it has been moved by an outside agency, and you drop a ball where you think your original ball came to rest, you dropped a ball in the wrong place. The penalty is LOHIMP. In stroke play you incurred a stroke and distance penalty plus an additional penalty of two strokes for playing from a wrong place. The breach was a serious one so you would be subject to disqualification unless you corrected your error.

LOHIMP = loss of hole in match play
TSISP = two strokes in stroke play

32
YOUR SCORECARD

o   On your scorecard you are responsible for entering your name and handicap and for ensuring that the gross score at each hole has been correctly entered by your marker.

o   If the Committee fails to provide a marker for a competition you may request a player in a friendly game to become your marker, but you must get the Committee's authority retrospectively.

o   Your marker must accompany you throughout the round or your card is invalid, i.e. your marker cannot rest at the 14th tee while you play 12 and 13 on your own.

o   If you enter the scores in the wrong place and re-number the holes on the card, the card is acceptable.

o   Alterations to a score card do not need to be initialled.

o   If your marker has lost your card, a duplicate may be made out, signed and returned.

o   Your card is not invalid if you and your marker sign the card in the wrong place. The card must have two signatures somewhere on it.

o   You may initial the scorecard rather than record your usual signature.

o   You must sign both cards in a 36 hole competition. Failure to do so would result in disqualification.

o   You must return your card to the Committee promptly after completion of the round. Delay could result in disqualification.

LOHIMP = loss of hole in match play
TSISP = two strokes in stroke play

o   If your marker leaves the course without returning your scorecard, you are permitted to fill out another card without the attestation of a marker if the Committee so allows.

o   Once your card has been signed, you cannot make any corrections by yourself. To do so would be to invalidate the attestation of the score by the marker. If the marker is not available, you may approach the Committee who may attest the correction.

o   You must complete the score for each hole. If you don't, but the total is correct, you are disqualified. It is the Committee's responsibility to add up the total score.

o   If you incorrectly add up the total score there is no penalty. Adding up the total is the Committee's responsibility.

o   If you start on the 10th hole make sure you mark the card for the 10-18 and not 1-9. If you don't you will be disqualified.

o   Make sure that the score recorded on the card is that of the competitor whose name is on the card. Cards do get swapped around inadvertently.

LOHIMP = loss of hole in match play
TSISP = two strokes in stroke play

33
THE HONOUR

o   In match play on a handicap basis, if you have the honour on the first tee but don't get a stroke and your opponent does, and you both score five, your opponent has the honour.

o   In stroke play on a handicap basis, the handicap is deducted at the end of the round and not at individual holes. The honour at the next tee is determined by the best gross score at the previous hole.

o   In a Stableford competition the reckoning is made as in match play and strokes are taken according to the handicap stroke table. The player with the better net score has the honour at the next tee.

34
THE BALL

o Make sure that your ball is uniquely identifiable before starting from the first tee. A ball which might be used as a provisional ball should not have the same marking as the ball you play with (see Sections 24 and 25 for the implications).

o If you play one stroke with a ball which does not meet the prescribed specifications you will be disqualified. Check that balls with XXXX across the maker's name are legal.

o If your ball breaks into pieces as a result of your stroke, you must replay the stroke without penalty.

o If your ball breaks into pieces as a result of striking a paved path, it is deemed to have broken as a result of your stroke and you must replay the stroke without penalty.

o You cannot use a handwarmer to warm your ball, this is deemed to be assistance. (You can use a handwarmer to warm your hands.)

o If you think your ball acted erratically and you examine it for damage and find none, you cannot change the ball.

o If you declare a ball unfit for play at a certain hole and substitute another ball, you can subsequently play the damaged ball without penalty. However you cannot declare it unfit (in the same condition) for play again.

o If you announce your intention of lifting your ball to check for damage and declare it unfit for play but your marker or opponent disputes the claim, if you substitute another ball you will be penalised LOHIMP or TSISP and you must hole out with the substituted ball.

LOHIMP = loss of hole in match play
TSISP = two strokes in stroke play

o   If you miss-hit a ball onto a green, then mark and lift the ball and declare it unfit for play and throw it into a pond but don't announce your intention you would be penalised LOHIMP or TSISP and you can substitute another ball to complete the hole.

35
CLUBS

o   If before the start of a round you discover that there are 15 clubs in your bag, discard one by taking it into the Clubhouse or your car. If you declare one of them out of play then start the round, you will be disqualified for carrying, during a round, an excess club declared out of play before the round.

o   You cannot carry a non-conforming club, even though you do not use it. The penalty is disqualification.

o   A club which conforms when new is deemed to conform after wear through normal use. A piece of material in the head of a metal wood which rattles due to use is still legal.

o   During a round you can put Band-Aid or a strip of tape on the top of a clubhead to reduce glare. It would not alter the playing characteristics of the club.

o   If you alter the playing characteristics of a club, for example through banging it against your foot (in disgust) and carry on playing with it, you will be disqualified.

o   During the play of a round you cannot apply chalk to the face of an iron club in order to obtain more backspin.

o   If you spit on the face of your club and do not wipe it off you will be disqualified.

o   You cannot change clubs during a round if the grips become wet.

o   If the grip on one of your clubs becomes loose during a round you can replace the club as it is deemed unfit for play.

o   You can wrap a towel or handkerchief around the grip of a club.

o   If you use your putter as a cane while climbing a hill and the shaft breaks, you may replace it during the round. The club is deemed to have been broken accidentally.

o   If you started a round with less than 14 clubs you may replace any club which has become unfit for play even if it is due to being broken in anger.

o   If you damage your putter by striking the ground with it, even if that is a normal habit, you cannot replace it. You should not subject a club to a strain which damages it.

o   If you lost your putter and you had started with 14 clubs, you cannot replace it. A lost club is not one which has become unfit for play in the normal course of play.

o   You can change clubs during the play of the two rounds in a 36 hole competition. The prohibition on changing clubs is during the play of a stipulated round.

o   If you break a club during a round and finish the round with 13 clubs, then find you are in a sudden death play-off, you can replace the broken club since the play-off constitutes a new round.

o   You cannot carry a weighted training club in addition to the 14 clubs selected for a round. You can carry it if you only have 13 clubs and if it conforms.

o   If you find another player's club on the course and put it in your bag containing 14 clubs, you are not deemed to have carried 15 clubs.

o   In stroke play, if you discover during the play of the eighth hole that you are carrying 15 clubs, you are penalised four strokes. These are added to your score at the first and second holes.

LOHIMP = loss of hole in match play
TSISP = two strokes in stroke play

o   If you leave your putter at the previous green, don't borrow your opponent's or fellow competitor's putter. The penalty is LOHIMP or TSISP for each hole at which the putter was borrowed with a maximum deduction of two holes or four strokes.

o   If your club breaks during the backswing and you complete the swing but miss the ball, you are not deemed to have made a stroke, since a stroke is the forward movement of the club and a shaft on its own is not a club.

o   If your clubhead separates from the shaft during the downswing and even though no contact is made with the ball, you are deemed to have made a stroke.

o   If the shaft of your club breaks during the downswing and you stop the swing but the clubhead falls onto the ball, there is a one stroke penalty if the ball was in play and the ball must be replaced. There is no penalty if the ball was on the tee. You did not make a stroke.

o   If the shaft of your club breaks during the downswing and you continue and miss the ball but the clubhead falls and moves the ball, you must play the ball as it lies without penalty. The stroke counts, however.

o   You can play a stroke with the back of the head of a club, i.e. playing left-handed with a right-handed club.

LOHIMP = loss of hole in match play
TSISP = two strokes in stroke play

36
THE PLAYER

o   You are responsible for knowing the conditions under which a competition is to be played:

–   handicap allocation (full, 2/3, 3/4)

–   format (singles, four-ball, foursome)

–   whether handicap is allocated by hole

o   Ensure that, in match play, you play the correct format. If you intentionally play foursome instead of four-ball or vice versa, you will be disqualified.

o   Ensure that you determine handicaps before starting a match. If not, you could find that you do not receive a handicap stroke where you are due one.

o   Ensure you know which holes you give or receive a handicap stroke. If you deviate from the handicap stroke table intentionally you would be disqualified; if you deviate mistakenly there is no penalty.

As above, if you state on the tee that you get a stroke when you don't, this is not wrong information and your opponent can't claim the hole when he realises you were incorrect. It is the responsibility of both players to know the holes at which handicap strokes are to be given or received.

o   If you have conceded a hole and then you realise you had a stroke, the concession stands.

o   If you mistakenly state a handicap higher than your true handicap (because your handicap has been adjusted) and a match is played

LOHIMP = loss of hole in match play
TSISP = two strokes in stroke play

on that basis, if you win, the result stands. No claim by your opponent can be considered unless you had knowingly given wrong information.

o   If you mistakenly play a match with full difference in handicap, instead of two-thirds or three-quarters, as required by the competition, the result of the match would stand.

o   If you mistakenly play in a stroke play event off a handicap higher than your real handicap (because it had been adjusted) and it is not noticed until after the competition has closed, the result stands. If it is noticed before the competition closes you would be disqualified, as you would if you knowingly played off a higher handicap.

o   In a greensome or foursome stroke play competition you must record each player's handicap on the scorecard. If you only record the combined handicap you will be disqualified.

o   Two players playing in the same competition at different times in the same day may caddie for each other.

o   In a stroke play competition a lone competitor would normally be allocated a marker by the committee. In the absence of a committee member, the competitor could organise his own marker.

o   Your marker must accompany you over the complete course in order for your card to be acceptable.

o   Remember to sign your scorecard. If you don't you will be disqualified.

o   If the committee allocates you a marker, i.e. only two players are playing and a spectator joins you, the spectator cannot mark either card. If he does you will be disqualified.

LOHIMP = loss of hole in match play
TSISP = two strokes in stroke play

o   In a stroke play competition, if the Committee issue you with a scorecard already containing your handicap in addition to your name and the competition date, you can not leave the handicap as written if it is incorrectly written as being higher than your actual handicap. Penalty is disqualification.

o   If the stakes in a water hazard have been improperly installed and your ball is outside the line of stakes but obviously in the water hazard you cannot claim it to be in casual water. The natural boundary of the water hazard should be recognised.

o   If a member of a following group plays a ball into your group, don't, in anger, hit the ball back towards the group. The penalty is LOHIMP or TSISP.